TENNESSEE WILLIAMS
AND FILM

TENNESSEE WILLIAMS AND FILM

Maurice Yacowar

Frederick Ungar Publishing Co.
New York

Copyright ©1977 by Frederick Ungar Publishing Co., Inc.
Printed in the United States of America
Designed by Anita Duncan

Library of Congress Cataloging in Publication Data

Yacowar, Maurice.
  Tennessee Williams and film.

  (Ungar film library)
  Filmography: p.
  Bibliography: p.
  Includes index.
  1. Williams, Tennessee, 1911-   —Film
adaptations. I. Title.
PS3545.I5365Z95   791.43'7   77-75335
ISBN 0-8044-2992-8
ISBN 0-8044-6990-3 pbk

To my wife, with love and thanks

Acknowledgments

I wish to thank the Canada Council and Brock University for the sabbatical and research grants that enabled me to write this book. My special thanks are due to Barbara Humphreys and her staff in the Motion Picture Section of the Library of Congress, Washington, D.C., without whose help and facilities this study would not have been possible.

Contents

Contents

Introduction

The movies were an important source of fantasy for Tennessee Williams in his childhood: "I used to want to climb into the screen and join the action. My mother had to hold me down."[1] How the movies sustained him in his later years we can infer from Tom Wingfield, his autobiographical surrogate in *The Glass Menagerie*. Tom goes to the movies at every opportunity to escape his mother's nagging and to bring adventure into his dreary life. But he realizes the danger:

> People go to the *movies* instead of *moving!* Hollywood characters are supposed to have all the adventures for everybody in America.... I'm tired of the *movies* and I am about to *move!* (p. 76)*

Actually, the movies helped Williams move—into the profession of writing. As a boy, he won $10 in a Saint Louis newspaper contest for a review of the silent *Stella Dallas*. He was an usher at the Strand (for $17 weekly) when Audrey Wood got him a job writing for Metro-Goldwyn-Mayer in Hollywood (a six-month contract at $250 weekly). The die was cast.

Williams did not make an auspicious debut in Hollywood. His first project—*The Sun Is My Undoing*—was canceled im-

*Quotations from Williams's works are from the printed versions listed in the bibliography.

mediately. The studio rejected his next contribution, to Lana Turner's role in *Marriage Is a Private Affair*. Assigned to help write a Margaret O'Brien script, Williams was relieved of the duty when he remarked upon his allergy to child stars. His salary continued, however, enabling him to write a film script called "The Gentleman Caller." When MGM rejected the script, Williams rewrote it as the play *The Glass Menagerie*. Soon the major studios were bidding for the rights to film Williams's first theatrical success.

Williams's early writing reveals his devotion to film. He wrote his early play *Stairs to the Roof* (1941) for production either on stage or on screen; the character of Benjamin D. Murphy was written with film star Burgess Meredith in mind. Similarly, Williams dedicated his one-act *Portrait of a Madonna* (1946) to Lillian Gish, and wrote another one-actor, *Last of My Solid Gold Watches* (1943), for Sidney Greenstreet. Indeed, the character Gutman that Greenstreet played in the John Huston film, *The Maltese Falcon* (1948), may be the character Gutman that Williams wrote into *Camino Real* (1948): "a lordly fat man wearing a linen suit and pith helmet," with a white cockatoo on his wrist! The film figure would be at home in a cast that included Casanova, Lord Byron, Don Quixote, and Kilroy.

Williams was drawn to write for the screen. He wrote a screenplay for Garbo in 1947, *The Pink Bedroom*, but she declined to come out of retirement. He was an unpaid and uncredited writer on Luchino Visconti's *Senso* (1954). Although *Baby Doll* is Williams's only realized work written expressly for the screen, Williams did work on the screen adaptations of *The Glass Menagerie*, *A Streetcar Named Desire*, *The Rose Tattoo*, *Suddenly Last Summer*, *The Fugitive Kind*, *Night of the Iguana*, and *BOOM*—with varying degrees of authority.

Film also proved an important influence upon his theater techniques. The liveliness of the popular American film may have been in his mind when, in his preface to *The Glass Menagerie*, he announced his "conception of a new, plastic theater which must take the place of the exhausted theater of realistic conventions if the theater is to resume vitality as a part of our culture" (p. ix). We find several filmic devices in this play. He proposed flashing titles on a screen to bridge the scenes or to define the characters' moods, after the manner of the silent cinema. His use of a spotlight upon Laura and upon the portrait of her father recalls film maker D.W. Griffith's use of the iris to frame off a segment of the total scene for emphasis. Later, Williams used a giant screen for the political rally in the stage production of *Sweet Bird of Youth*. He sets the stage for *This Property Is Condemned* with a series of precise, evocative visual details that seem to invite filming.

More generally, Williams's writing style was influenced by film. For instance, in his stage dialogue he avoided theatrical diction in preference for the naturalism established in American film. Then, too, he rarely wrote plays in the traditional structure by acts. Instead, as he directed in the production notes for *Summer and Smoke,* "Everything possible should be done to give an unbroken fluid quality to the sequence of scenes"(p. 10). *Camino Real* may be his most filmic play, with its "continually dissolving and transforming images of a dream"(pp. vi-vii). Williams has even referred to the short scenes of his theater by the film term, "takes."[2] So from film Williams drew many of the tones, devices, and rhythms that distinguish his theater. Certainly the films he watched fed that "great vocabulary of images" that Williams—in his preface to *Camino Real* (p. viii)—suggests is the conscious and unconscious source of all one's communication and dreams.

Finally, film helped Williams reach a wider audience. He has often written of his desire to "reach out /his/ arms and embrace the whole world."[3] In his preface to *Cat on a Hot Tin Roof* he quotes his earlier statement:

> I have never for one moment doubted that there are people—millions!—to say things to.... It is the short reach of my arms that hinders, not the length and multiplicity of theirs. (*p.101*)

The films of Williams's plays increased the audience, as this warmest and most intimate of playwrights craved. Often his films played in communities that had not seen stage productions of his work. It may well be that Williams is most widely known for the fifteen feature films that have been made of his works, from *The Glass Menagerie* through *Last of the Mobile Hot-shots*.

How well has Williams weathered the adaptation? How accurate is one's sense of Williams if it comes from his films? Before we consider these questions, we might pause to survey the problems inherent in filming a play.

It seems that any study of adaptation becomes a study of compromise. There are, broadly speaking, three areas of compromise involved in the translation of a play or novel to the screen: the formal differences between the media involved, the social context, and the matter of the director's intervention.

Firstly, the theater experience of a work differs from the film experience. Most of the differences in form relate to the physical realism of the film image of life, as against the artificiality of the stage image. We see representative props in a stage production, but in a film we have an image of the real thing itself. As a consequence, a heightened form of "acting" is needed on stage, while "behaving"—the unobtrusive gestures of real life—is required in film. Then, too, the actor is the expressive center on stage, while in film the actor is only a part of the expressive whole; the significance is as likely to emerge from the lighting, set, props, sound effects, or camera angle, as from the actor's speech or gesture.

The mobility of the camera makes for other differences between the media. In theater we have a single, fixed perspective upon the action, which predisposes us to an objective stance. But because the film camera can crawl and soar, it gives us a variety of points of view, in both the physical and emotional senses of the phrase. The film experience therefore tends to be the more subjective.

We even perceive the actor in a different way. In theater the actor is another physical presence, as is the viewer, but in film the actor is an image. The viewer can identify more intensely with the image of the actor than with the actor who is physically present.[4] Again, the film experience is the more subjective.

Moreover, in film acting as opposed to theater performance, an actor tends to develop a continuing persona after a number of roles. We may speak of an actor personalizing a role—the Wolfit Lear, the Scofield Macbeth—but this is a matter of style. We never speak of a stage actor developing a consistent image across a number of roles; that would not be what in theater is called "acting." Yet in film this is a common phenomenon. The most distinctive film actors develop a continuous image, which can be inflected in an individual work, but which remains consistent over a number of roles. Most actors whom we consider "film stars" will likely have developed a persona. As specific examples, the recent work of John Wayne and Henry Fonda depends upon their images and the values that have accrued to those images over the years. Or again: one would analyze a stage production of a Samuel Beckett play without reference to the actors' previous roles, but an analysis of Beckett's film *Film* must take into account the face of Buster Keaton, an actor with a full and precise complex of associations from other films. If it does not, the analysis will have omitted the dominant element in both the language and the plot of the work. This continuity of the film star's image is the aesthetic source of the star system, typecasting, and (true) the disdain in which the purest film "acting" is held by those who apply the criteria of stage performance. In a film adaptation, then, the dialogue may prove less expressive than the persona, the external associations, of the actor delivering the dialogue.

Secondly, there are the differences attributable to the social context in which the media operate. Differences may be simple, such as the tradition of intermissions in theater but not in film. To put the matter more generally, a play is tradi-

tionally developed as a series of separate segments, whereas
a film is a continuous flow of action. Then, too, films are run
several times an evening, with audiences coming and going at
all times, eating, drinking, and chatting with something less
than the reverence that the theatrical "event" enjoys. This
may mean that a film cannot expect the intense concentration
that a playwright assumes of his audience.

Thus, film is a mass medium, while theater still is regarded as the interest of a small, sophisticated minority. One
practical consequence of this attitude is that film in America
has always lagged behind theater in permissiveness of language and theme. Adjusting controversial subject matter to
the decorum of the mass audience has always been one of the
most difficult compromises for adapters to make.

It should also be remembered that the verbal element
dominates the visual in theater, whereas the visual is pre-
dominant in film. The word need not be subordinate in film,
but it tends to be, perhaps because audiences have not culti-
vated their aural attention and verbal receptivity, or because
film artists have preferred striking visual effects over subtler
verbal ones. In any case, it remains the adapter's responsibility to reduce the verbal density of a play and to seek visual
equivalents.

Thirdly, there is the compromise that seems the inevitable consequence of one artist producing the text of another.
In any presentation of a play, whether on stage or on screen,
the director can take liberties with the text. The playwright's
instructions can be tempered or ignored. Even more latitude
is allowed the director when the author has not specified his
directions. The pronunciation of a phrase, the accent on a
word, the tone of a syllable, the placement of the characters—even in details as small as these can a text be inflected,
or even subverted.

There is even more latitude for individual interpretation
in filming. Whole sections of the action can be omitted by a
close-up, for example, or a peripheral reaction can be emphasized by one. Whole scenes can be omitted so that the three

hours traffic of the stage can be compressed into the conventional ninety minutes of the feature film.

In addition to all these changes, which may be made to adjust to the differences between the media or the differences in interpretation, other alterations may be necessary in the interests of fidelity to the original. Most obviously, a film may open out the action in order to avoid the impression that a restricted atmosphere is part of the import of the play. For while a single set is natural in theater, it is uncommon in film.

The faithful adaptation will convey the spirit, meaning, and importance of the original work, even if it means taking liberties with the surface of the play, with the plot and characters. Good adaptation is not one that makes no changes, but one in which the changes serve the intention and thrust of the original. As a result, judging an adaptation is as delicate and dangerous a business as making one. For the critic has two creations for which he must work past the form to the spirit, and he must suspend his response to the original, in order to make a reasonable judgment.

1

The Glass Menagerie
(1950)

The first Tennessee Williams film can serve as a textbook demonstration of how insensitive compromises can ruin an adaptation. Williams conceived *The Glass Menagerie* in a nonnaturalistic mode, with expressionistic lighting and music and with a filmic flow of short scenes. But filmic elements in a theatrical production may not work the same way when used in a film; for one thing, the surprise is gone. Perhaps an extremely theatrical device might be necessary in a film, for equivalence to a filmic device on stage. In any case, Williams seemed to forestall any filming of the play, when he cited in his production notes "the unimportance of the photographic in art." Reality is "an organic thing which the poetic imagination can represent, or suggest, in essence, only through transformation" (p. ix). The scene, we are told, is memory and therefore unrealistic, omitting some details and emphasizing others, "according to the emotional value" of the material, for "memory is seated predominantly in the heart" (p. 3). But film is seated predominantly in the physical reality. In the film of *The Glass Menagerie*, the poetic spirit of the original is sacrificed to the literal realism of a conventional romantic film.

In the play, Laura Wingfield is a shy, crippled girl who collects glass animals as a refuge from the demands and shocks of the outside world. Her mother Amanda is a vain Southern belle who hoards fantasies of success and nags her

9

children until they try to escape her—Laura to her menagerie, son Tom to the life of a wandering sailor. Tom seems
modeled after Williams himself, an aspiring poet who works
in a shoe warehouse and finally flees his family. The action
centers around the dinner visit of Jim O'Connor, Tom's friend
from work, whom Amanda takes to be a possible suitor for
Laura. But Jim is engaged. The evening ends with Amanda's
hopes dashed and Laura's favorite glass piece, a unicorn,
with its horn broken off, now just an ordinary horse.

The primary failure of the film was the producers' insistence upon a happy ending.[1] Where the play dramatized the
impossibility of achieving one's dreams (Amanda, Jim) or of
escaping one's limits either physical (Laura) or emotional
(Tom), the film affirms the shallow confidence of O'Connor.
Laura is not left lonely and abandoned, as in the play; instead, we last see her as a happy, well-adjusted girl, coolly
awaiting her own gentleman caller.

Consistent with this recovery, Laura is normalized
throughout the film. In the play she was pathologically shy,
too shy even to go to her typing class. In the film she bravely
goes to class but is—justifiably—repelled by a cruel teacher
and an excessively difficult exam. Thus Williams's hypersensitive creature is transformed into a patient, reasonable
girl who is offended beyond endurance.

Director Irving Rapper altered the material to enhance
Laura's normalcy. For example, in Williams's opening scene,
Amanda confronts Laura with her truancy and lying. But this
scene does not occur until the middle of the film. Williams's
powerful scene of character revelation is thus reduced to
trivial suspense over whether or not Laura will be caught in
her truancy. Moreover, the footage of Laura's visits to the zoo
suggests that she is enjoying herself, not that she is wandering
lonely and homeless, as in the play.

The film diminishes the imaginative hold that Laura has
on Tom, by making her seem just a normal girl. In the play,
Tom remains haunted by Laura's memory. He feels guilty for
having abandoned her. But in the film Laura gently sends

Tom off on his way; she can manage without him. In the play, Tom's recollection was forced by the strength of Laura's presence in his mind. In the film, Tom begins by complaining about the boredom of a sailor on dog watch. From idleness, not from obsession, does his mind turn to his Laura.

Actually, the film reduces the complexity of all the major characters. Amanda loses honor and her aristocratic unworldliness when the film shows her quarreling over an unpaid bill in a department store. Similarly, Tom's dreams of adventure are reduced to an exotic lie told to confuse a pickup in a bar. But, with the exception of Laura, the worst casualty is Jim O'Connor. In the play, Jim is a subtle example of failure, the high-school hero who sustains his optimism despite his failure to realize his promise. Williams presents him as a charming, simple fellow. But in the film, Jim is played as a hero. He glibly maneuvers his foreman and colleagues. Gone is his veneration of the inventor of chewing gum! The only trace of irony in O'Connor's character in the film is the fact that his longest chat with Tom occurs in the men's washroom. The irony fails because the scene still suggests that the figure is superior to his surroundings, not—as in the play—subdued by them.

The film also omits Jim's double service as Romantic Dream and—as Tom introduces him—as "the most realistic character in the play, being an emissary from a world of reality that we were somehow set apart from" (p. 5). First, the Romance. In the play, Laura first mentions Jim to Amanda as a boy she admired in high school. For one shocking moment, then, his appearance seems to be the miraculous fulfillment of her dreams. This makes her ultimate disappointment all the greater. The film omits the confiding in Amanda, so Laura's involvement with Jim is simplified.

Nor does Jim serve as an "emissary from reality," because the film shows the Wingfield family in the outside world of reality. Laura is at home in the zoo, Amanda in the stores, and Tom in the streets and bars. By opening out the action, the film dissipates the play's sense of oppressive confinement in the Wingfield apartment. Irving Rapper actually reverses the values of the play when he has Jim step in from the rain (a trademark of Rapper's films), thereby suggesting that the Wingfield apartment is a comfortable haven. It is not. In this instance the "freedom" of the camera violated the play's tension for escape.

Other, minor insensitivities abound in the film. Laura is shown buying her unicorn en route to her typing class. In the play she had treasured that piece for thirteen years. Again, the film simplifies Laura's emotion. The broken unicorn is no longer Laura's long-time favorite, indeed her emblem; it is just a piece of glass. In the play Jim whirls Laura around for a short dance in the living room, causing the unicorn to break, while in the film the dance is made public, at the hall across the alley. The film here disrupts the delicate balance between privacy and exposure in Williams's scene.

Rapper also violates the consistency of Tom's perspective upon the action. Often the film shows us what Tom did not see, and so could not remember in a memory play. Amanda's memory of her success with seventeen gentleman callers at a ball is the most striking example. Firstly, Rapper shows the scene as an event, not as a story, so he eliminates the possibility that the tale is Amanda's invention. Secondly, we see it as a part of what Tom sees or experiences throughout the film, although the scene is Amanda's memory, not Tom's. Finally, Rapper's Amanda kisses a number of the men, a detail in conflict with Amanda's pretense to romantic gentility. Similarly, the subjective shot of Laura limping loudly to her desk is outside Tom's experience; it is a striking effect but it disturbs the logic of the drama.

In addition to these minor difficulties, the film fails to develop an equivalent for the poetic techniques of the play. For example, in the play the expressionistic lighting of Laura suggests her apartness from the others, even a luminosity in her spirit. In the film Laura is lit naturalistically, so her character loses much of its poetic effect. Similarly, the portrait of Tom's father lights up from time to time in the play, again expressing the strong character of the man who fled the family and who remains a lively example to Tom. When the father figures in the conversation or thought of the film, Rapper provides the traditional close-up or keeps the picture in focus behind the characters. The general effect is the same: the portrait is emphasized. But replacing a surprising stage effect with a familiar film device produces a less exciting style (and in this case reduces the strength of the father's image).

Only once does the film reach for the expressionistic lighting of the play. When Jim leaves the Wingfields, a white-wall tire in front of the alley flahes on and off, catching the lights from the dance hall. This is a clever shot but it fails in logic: the image of tempting mobility should be associated with Tom's escape, not Jim's. And the devices of luminous representation should be associated with Laura and the father, as in the play, not with a tire on a stranger's car.

In addition to these failures in script and in filming, the cast of big names did not meet the artistic needs of the play. Laura's fragility and delicacy are lost in the vigor, solidity, and discretion that characterized Jane Wyman's persona as The Indomitable Sufferer from *Johnny Belinda* (1948) on. Gertrude Lawrence was a compromise casting—Rapper wanted Tallulah Bankhead—and she proved too earthy for Amanda, too ready with wink or haggard grimace. The role of faded Southern flower was not within Lawrence's easy range, and the script and Rapper's direction rendered it remoter still. Thus, the film makes Amanda even more strident than the play ("You're not crippled! Walk, Laura.... I want to see you walk!"). The development of Laura's relationship with Jim is continually interrupted by shots of Amanda mugging at Tom. Finally, Kirk Douglas performs well as Jim, but his persona is too hearty, energetic, likable, and affluent to express the sham success of Williams's O'Connor. The play's simple failure becomes in the film a hero of substance and style.

By providing this simple "hero" and by giving Laura a happy romantic ending, the film relates to the original play—as the horse does to the unicorn. Something distinctive

and extremely personal has been converted into something
simple and prosaic, the standard romantic melodrama. Williams rightly declares it "the most awful travesty of the play
I've ever seen ... horribly mangled by the people who did the
film-script."[2]

2

A Streetcar Named Desire

(1951)

The film of *A Streetcar Named Desire* grew directly out of the New York stage production (which opened on December 3, 1947), so it escaped the kinds of subversion that *The Glass Menagerie* suffered on the screen. Williams wrote the screenplay with Elia Kazan, who directed both the stage and film productions. Virtually the entire cast was retained for the movie, including leads Marlon Brando, Kim Hunter, and Karl Malden. But as Blanche, Jessica Tandy was replaced by Vivien Leigh, from Laurence Olivier's London production, at the producers' insistence upon at least one box-office name. Leigh's casting did not compromise the film.

Two types of illusion clash in *A Streetcar Named Desire*. Blanche DuBois is the penniless romantic ruin who struggles to maintain her illusions of beauty and romance in the face of aging and disappointment. Her husband killed himself when she taunted him for his homosexuality. Now she is lonely. For seducing a student, she has been fired from her teaching job. She comes to seek refuge with her younger sister Stella.

Stella's husband is Stanley Kowalski—brute health and physicality embodied in a vulgar, violent man. If Blanche's illusion is the survival of beauty and innocence, Kowalski's illusion is that human nature consists exclusively of physical reality. Blanche poses a threat to the physical and emotional hold that Kowalski has on Stella. To Stanley, Stella is a sen-

15

sual woman; to Blanche, she is a remote "star," as even her name suggests.

Stanley is a double threat to Blanche. He ruins her hopes of winning Mitch, a sad bachelor devoted to his sick mother, by telling Mitch about Blanche's sordid past. Then, while Stella is in the hospital having a baby, Kowalski rapes Blanche, driving her into insanity. Stanley has forced Blanche back into the sordid physicality that she had sought to gloss over in her imagination.

The play ends with Blanche taken away to an asylum, Stanley continuing his brutish diversions, and Stella forcing herself to doubt Blanche's accusations, in order to be able to live with her husband. Her instincts confirm Blanche's charges, but Stella, too, needs an illusion to sustain her life and love.

The film moves even more inexorably than the play toward the clash between Blanche's romantic illusions and Kowalski's brutish, though affable, realism. In the play, the audience has time to savor Blanche's brief confidence about winning Mitch ("Sometimes—there's God—so quickly!"). There is an intermission before the scene in which Blanche waits in vain for Mitch to arrive. Between her glimpse of salvation and her disappointment, then, Blanche has some breathing time. But in the film, Kazan dissolves from Blanche's hopeful line to the factory, where Mitch attacks Stanley for his sordid report about Blanche. There is no peace for Blanche, not even a moment of hope. The film then plunges directly to Kowalski's physical triumph over Blanche's fragile dreams, as expressed by the rape.

Kazan has remarked that if he were to remake the film he would do whole scenes more calmly and slowly,[1] but at the time of its release, the film's grim thrust was a powerful experience. Kazan concentrated the tensions through abundant close-ups, and he made the set seem smaller as the drama progressed, as Kowalski's world closed in upon Blanche, by removing the flooring platforms (flats) and bringing his camera in closer, pinning the characters in the corners of the cramped, peeling apartment.

To help preserve the compression of the play, and the cramped, stifling mood of Stanley's apartment, Kazan abandoned his earlier plans to open out the action. He did add some exterior scenes, but none involved extensive padding of the text; they were generally new settings for scenes in the play. Moreover, none of the additions were merely ornamental. Rather, the shots of the outside world provided physical metaphors for Blanche's mental state. For Blanche is the central figure in the play, Kazan noted during the original stage production,[2] and so Kazan's shots of the outside world are projections of her mental state.

For example, where the play opens on the Kowalski tenement, the film begins with Blanche emerging from a cloud of engine steam in the New Orleans train station. This introduction makes Blanche our first figure for identification (and thereby, sympathy). Moreover, the scene introduces the basic elements that characterize Blanche's suffering throughout the film.

First, the steam and the sweating crowds of jostling strangers set up the heat motif. Blanche cannot escape the discomfort of heat, emblematic both of her own sensuality and of the pressure of other people's presence upon her. Kowalski sweats from his physical enthusiasms. Mitch sweats from his tensions, as he wavers between Kowalski's vision and Blanche's. Fever pervades the film. Even neighbor Eunice is associated with the pattern, as she threatens the cardplayers with a kettle of boiling water. Paradoxically, Blanche's refuge from the heat is hot baths; similarly, her romanticism leads her to satisfy her sensuality, as well as to flee it.

The second of Blanche's pressures introduced in the train station is noise, which the screenplay describes as "filtered into a sonic abstraction"[3] to underline its metaphoric function. Almost every scene begins with the noise of street life.

When she confides in Stella, Blanche tries to seal out the noise with shutters, but the outside world is too strong for her. Later, the noise of the passing trains shakes the apartment and drives her outside. When she is not tormented by the real noise, Blanche is haunted by the dance melody which played where her husband killed himself. Thus the noise is of two contrary types: the coarse sounds of her real environment and the maddening music of her sentimental memory. Blanche reacts to the noise as she does to the heat: paradoxically, she turns up the radio to drown out her surroundings.

Third, the railway scene introduces Blanche's discomfort in light. The passing train rakes her body with light and she recoils. Later Blanche prefers the shadows. She claims this to be virtuous: "I can't stand a naked light bulb," she tells Mitch, "any more than I can a rude remark or a vulgar action." The Chinese lantern she has Mitch attach over her light becomes a symbol of her desire to cover exposing light with shadowing ornament. Actually, Blanche seeks to conceal her age and decay. Hiding the physical truth allows her romantic fantasies to flourish: "I don't want realism, I want magic!" In her final confrontation with Mitch, Blanche's dark room is violated by the flickering neon sign outside. This light, like Mitch's attack, is more sordid than Blanche's deception. Moreover, Blanche has been photographed in soft focus, so when Mitch forces her face under the naked light, the sudden clarity is shocking—and Blanche's exposure an anticipation of Kowalski's rape.

In contrast to Blanche's defensive and romantic preference for the shadows, Kowalski has a robust enthusiasm for darkness. On his wedding night he "rushed about the place smashing the light bulbs" with Stella's slippers. He still holds Stella by the "colored lights" of their love-making. But Kowalski's rape and subsequent denial of it are deeds of darkness that make Blanche's wistful refuge in the shadows all the more touching.

Blanche's final pressure in the railway station is the buffeting by other people. Throughout the film, she suffers from contact with others. For example, she misses privacy in her corner of Kowalski's room. Mitch is both shy and sensitive to her needs when he dances with her, standing apart, not touching. The pressure of other presences points to the impossibility of Blanche's fantasies surviving coarse reality. Occasionally, the real world offers up someone of gentleness, like the newspaper boy (probably enhanced by Blanche's romantic fancy). And in the railway station there is the handsome young sailor, who whistles what Blanche would dearly love to be able to sing, "Somebody Loves Me." By showing the sailor helping Blanche, Kazan anticipates Blanche's later remark to the doctor who takes her away: "Whoever you are—I have always depended on the kindness of strangers." The scene with the sailor confirms Blanche's claim. Kowalski's vision of life, of course, admits of no such open trust or vulnerability.

But for the most part, people intrude into Blanche's life. The traveling salesmen spread her disrepute, for example. Kazan's scenes of public buffeting and noise show Blanche's discomfort and suggest the privacy that her fantasy needs in order to survive. The crowd scenes culminate in Kazan's addition to the scene where Mitch rejects Blanche and then assaults her. She chases him from the room and rushes out to the square. The neighbors come out to watch her weeping there. Observers call the police. But in the cold high-angle shot, when the camera looks down at the cowering Blanche, we see that Kowalski's gossip and Mitch's acceptance of it have reduced the dreamer to the squalor of the tenement square. This scene is Blanche's most public exposure and from it she retreats to her most intense fantasy, that she has been invited away by an old beau.

Kazan exploits the mobility of his medium here to visualize the conflict between Blanche's fantasies and the oppressive reality that finally overwhelms her. The smoke, heat, noise, and jostling bodies are the physical pressures that Kowalski embodies and that Blanche's imagination seeks to gloss.

Kazan's other major addition is to the rape scene. The struggle between Blanche and Stanley is shot in reflection through a large, oval mirror. Blanche's last defense, a broken bottle, shatters the mirror. The solid object (bottle, Kowalski) shatters the fragile image (mirror, Blanche). The mirror is an image of Blanche's shattered composure and self-respect. There is also a horror in the shot, as if it were too powerful to be viewed directly and needed to be deflected.

Kazan's next shot is an outrageous visual pun. A fire hose sprays the garbage off the street. The image has been set up by Eunice's earlier line to Stanley: "I hope they do haul you in and turn the fire hose on you, same as last time." But appearing immediately after the rape, the hose conveys an image of phallic forcefulness. The image contains multiple perspectives. As bawdry, it tempts us into Stanley's view, that the affected Blanche is trash, which needs to be washed away by his purifying, direct force. This sense agrees with the "raffish charm" that the screenplay (p.338) described in Kowalski's furnishings. From Blanche's perspective, however, the shot expresses her shame and the blow to her self-respect caused by the rape and then Stella's disbelief. Eunice's line gives the image yet another meaning; it suggests that Stanley, formerly a victim of the hose and treated as trash by the regularizing forces in society, is now enjoying a kind of revenge by bringing Blanche down to his level. Finally, the image relates to the succeeding scene, where we see the Kowalski baby in his carriage. From this perspective, the characters are washing aside the embarrassing past in order to begin life anew. At whatever cost to Blanche, of course.

Kazan's additions are shrewd visualizations of the themes of the play. He is also sensitive to textures. Stanley's thick, bulky build is contrasted to the fragility of Blanche. She spreads a lacy white thing as she flirts with Stanley ("I cannot imagine any witch of a woman casting a spell over you").

When we later see the Kowalski baby covered in a black net, we may feel that Blanche's influence continues, even after she has been taken away. Similarly, Kazan shifts the delicate Scene Six, in which Mitch and Blanche have their most promising romantic chat, from the Kowalski apartment to a pier dance hall, where Blanche can enjoy a brief calm and coolness. But from the moment Mitch asks her age she is shaken; so instead of a wall behind her, from that point she is shot against the open water, a single rail behind her head as an image of her lost support.

The film is as sensitive aurally as it is visually. When Blanche offers Mitch a drink, she says in a grating, masculine tone, "It isn't Stan's," then recovers her pose to say with ladylike softness, "Some things on the premises are actually mine!" Both the tone and the content of her speech show her struggling for self-possession. In her later madness, the order is reversed. She begins a line softly but ends it with a hard: "They! Who's 'they'?" Here her tones indicate the disintegration of her composure.

Kazan often directs his actors against the text. For example, when Stanley prepares to rape Blanche, he uses his gentlest tone for "All right, let's have some rough-house," because he knows he is in control. Similarly, Blanche asks Mitch about his mother. "You love her very much, don't you?" In the play Mitch answers "Yes." In Williams's screenplay, "Mitch nods miserably." But in Kazan's film, Mitch looks both ways tightly, as if afraid of being watched, before replying with a choked and wary nod. For he loves his mother but has evidently been teased for his devotion. Or, he loves her, but not without an unadmitted resentment at the sacrifices he has made for her. Or, he loves her but cannot say it; or he does not love her and cannot say that either. This is an example of Kazan's concern with the interior lives of his characters, which are often belied by their actions and speech.

Generally speaking, then, the film of *A Streetcar Named Desire* is a model of sensitive, faithful adaptation of a stage play to film. But there was one difficulty, and that was due to the social context. The play dealt with topics—insanity, nymphomania, rape, speculation about the nature of man—that were rather heady stuff for the American cinema of the early 1950s. At a time when American films were almost exclusively safe family entertainments, the film version of *A Streetcar Named Desire* was not to be easily received. Indeed it encountered severe difficulties with the censors.

To start with, innumerable small changes were made in the text to make the play more decorous. Stanley's "You're damn tootin'" becomes "You betcha life," for example. His call to Stella in the bathroom is sanitized from "Haven't fallen in, have you?" to "Whatja do, fall asleep in there?" These modifications are understandable in the transfer of text from Broadway to the mass audience and little is lost in the translation.

But more serious alterations were required due to pressure from the censor and from the Catholic Legion of Decency. The censor insisted on the removal of the hint that Blanche's first husband was homosexual. Kazan was amenable on this point, because he preferred the victim to be considered weak, rather than deviant. But when the censor required the removal of the rape scene, both Williams and Kazan opposed him adamantly.[4]

Williams and Kazan labored to find an acceptable compromise, but they refused to remove the rape scene, which they argued was the crux of the action. Finally it was agreed that the rape would remain but that the rapist would not go unpunished. The film ends with Stella rejecting Stanley ("Don't you touch me. Don't you ever touch me again.") and assuring her baby that "We're not going back in there. Not this time. We're never going back. Never, never back, never back again." This seemed to clear the film, except that Warner Brothers—without informing either the author or the director—made another twelve cuts to appease the Legion.[5]

As a result of the compromise, the conclusion of the film seems to be the reverse of that of the play. For the play ends with Blanche destroyed and Stella lying to herself: Stella collapses into Stanley's arms "with inhuman abandon" (p.142). As the curtain falls, Stanley unbuttons Stella's blouse and his brutish friends play on ("seven card stud," aptly enough). But the film ends with Stanley abandoned. Even his card cronies turn against him. Blanche, then, would seem to have won, for she has exposed Stanley and kept Stella from "hanging back with the brutes." As Blanche is driven away, against the silhouette of the cathedral, we hear the bells that she earlier called "the only clean thing in the quarter." Where in the play it seems that Stanley has won, in the film Blanche seems triumphant.

But the film's ending is closer to the play's than this difference would suggest. For one thing, Mitch is hypocritical in turning against Stanley, because it was Mitch who abandoned Blanche and attempted the rape that Kowalski later achieved. So Mitch is shown to live the kind of defensive lie that Stella does in the play. Moreover, Stella's last speech is undercut by several ironies. She expresses her resolve to leave to the baby, not to the rather more dangerous Stanley. And she does not leave the quarter, but just goes upstairs to Eunice's apartment; and Stanley's call had been enough to bring her back from Eunice's before. And in Stella's repetition of "nevers," did the lady perhaps protest too much? So the film's conclusion reverses the externals of the play, but not the bleak vision beneath. To the questioning viewer, the film ends as negatively as did the play.

As it happens, the compromise ending of the film may have been truer to Kazan's vision than the original ending, which showed life being sustained by a lie. Kazan rejected another ending Williams proposed for the film, in which Stella would have been seen crying.[6] It may well be that Kazan preferred the film's ending—in which a hard truth is openly faced—over the other two endings, which show a weak Stella either hiding a truth or crying because of it.

In his films, Kazan frequently presents the truth-teller in heroic terms: *On the Waterfront, A Face in the Crowd, The Harder They Fall.* In *Panic in the Streets,* keeping a secret proves fatal to the keeper and dangerous to the community. Kazan's concern with the ethics of the informer may relate back to the fact that he was one of the few liberal artists who consented to testify before the House Un-American Activities Committee investigation into Communist elements in the arts. Since then, he has often defended the unpopular position that he took. Thus it is consistent with Kazan's view that in A Streetcar Named Desire the truth is not kept secret, even within Stella's own mind, but is confronted, is believed, and —even if only temporarily—is the basis for her decision to leave her husband.

Williams recalls "the marvelous performances in [this] great movie, only slightly marred by Hollywood ending."[7] But the ending is richer in irony and in directorial inflection than the usual Hollywood ending. All in all, the film is as subtle and as powerful as the play. It is an invaluable record of a legendary production. It is also something of a landmark in American cinema. It introduced Method acting to the mass audience and it had the first major film score based on jazz. And in an age of simple family entertainments, A Streetcar Named Desire struck a blow for mature film making by assuming that there was an audience for serious, challenging cinema. Its success led to further explorations in adult film, although, sad to say, not many had the tact and the sensitivity of this pioneer.

3

The Rose Tattoo

(1955)

The film of *The Rose Tattoo* demonstrates how much more there is to adaptation than merely following the general outlines of plot and characterization. The story line and general character signification in the film are faithful to the play. But the film subverts the original in two basic ways: it scales down the passion and it simplifies the seriocomic complexity of Williams's play.

In one respect, the film is truer to Williams's intention than the original stage production (which opened on February 3, 1951) was. Williams wrote the lead role for Anna Magnani, but she was loath to undertake a demanding stage role in English, so the part went to Maureen Stapleton. Magnani was subsequently cast in the film, ensuring its European success, but to safeguard the American box-office, Burt Lancaster replaced Eli Wallach as Alvaro, the truckdriver. Lancaster's Italian is, sadly, a matter of grammar but not of lilt; his plausibility is constantly shaken by his flat *a*'s. The film was directed by Daniel Mann, who also directed the stage production. Williams's part in the travesty of the screen version is uncertain. He is credited for the screenplay, but Hal Kanter is credited for the "adaptation." Wherever the fault lies, the film is a hollowing of the play.

Williams's "love-play to the world"[1] is the story of Serafina Delle Rose, a passionate Sicilian seamstress living somewhere between New Orleans and Mobile. Serafina worships her huband Rosario, who is not seen in the play. On the night when she tells him that she is expecting their second child, he dies in a crash, while bootlegging for a nightclub. Serafina loses the child and retires to serve Rosario's memory. She even locks up the clothing of her teen-aged daughter Rosa to keep her from dishonoring the family name with a sailor.

Then Serafina learns that Rosario had been unfaithful to her. He had had an affair with Estelle Hohengarten, a gambler at the nightclub. Estelle had even tattooed a rose on her chest to match Rosario's rose tattoo. Serafina shatters the urn in which she had treasured Rosario's remains. She then accepts the love of a clownish, sentimental trucker, Alvaro Mangiacavallo, at first furtively, but then openly when she resolves to devote her passion to the living, not to the dead.

As was usual, the play was refined for the film audience. The neighbor's fulminations against "the Wops" were discreetly abbreviated or omitted. So too "Wop" became "macaroni," "Dago" became "Italian," "Catholic" became "respectable," and "buggers" became "monkeys." "Virgin" became "innocent—pure." And a contraceptive that accidentally falls from Alvaro's pocket in the play, bringing from Serafina the reproof, "Is that your poetry?" became a stolen kiss in the film.

By the logic of the play, that kiss would indeed have been poetry. An exuberant celebration of love, the play disdains time and loss for a love that soars beyond the formalities of marriage and the law. Passion is magical in the play. Thus Serafina has a vision of Rosario's rose on her breast when she conceives their children. The play also accepts the magic that man makes by himself. Estelle's and Alvaro's tattoos are prosaic but valid analogues to the miracle of Serafina's visions. In his preface, Williams affirms the validity of even the passing passion, that which declines into indifference. For "Snatching the eternal out of the desperately fleeting is the great magic trick of human existence" (p.9). Estelle, Rosario, and Alvaro perform this trick, by their open, intense loving. Serafina must overcome her demands for fidelity and eternity in order to do so. Then she can find a heroic romance even in a buffoon named "Eat-a-horse" (Mangiacavallo). The play, then, exalts the magic and the passion that can be generated even in a passing fancy or amid the prosaic elements of life.

But the film reduces the passionate to the mundane. Where the play exalted passion, the film values marriage. In the play Rosa rushes off for a night of love; in the film, for marriage and domesticity. In the following contrast, Alvaro's sense of the justice of passion is replaced by the stable logic of reproduction and family life:

> Sooner or later the innocence of your daughter cannot be respected.   *(Play, p.101)*

> Sooner or later the innocence of your daughter cannot be respected if the family's going to continue, you know. *(Film)*

Where in the play passion is its own end, in the film logic and marriage must justify love-making.

The characters are correspondingly reduced in the scale of their emotion and their liveliness. The play introduces Alvaro in a burst of violence; he is fired for fighting. In the film we first see him at a church bazaar; there he is fired for playing Bingo. Where in the play Serafina and Alvaro meet by fateful accident, in the film Alvaro's sister plots a match between them. Jack Hunter, Rosa's sailor, is reduced from a dashing earringed lover to a character with the emotional force of a newspaper boy (one, that is, untouched by the famished fantasy of a Blanche DuBois). The film Rosa is more aggressive sexually than Jack, yet in her quarrels with her mother, the film Rosa is tamer. She speaks rather gently the lines written for a spitfire:

> *[Violently:]* Mama, mama, su, Mama! She didn't sleep good last night.   (p.55)

> I didn't bring Jack here to be insulted.   (p.59)

Williams's passionate young lovers are subdued to the spirit of high-school guidance counselors. Reductionism pervades

the film, even in inconsequential matters. In the play Rosario
drives a ten-ton truck of bananas and Alvaro an eight-ton
truck; in the film the trucks weigh five and three tons respectively.

The poetry of the play is further subdued by the film's ex-
cessive visualization. Evocation can be more effective than
presentation. In the play Rosario is a haunting idea in Serafina's mind, because he is never seen on stage, never given a
corporeal reality. In the film Rosario is shown, a silent, surly
presence, his tattoo visible from the shadows, as he promises
to make no more night runs. His appearance costs him his
mystery. The film shows him speeding to his doom when he
sees Estelle and Serafina together, as if his death is to be tak-
en as punishment for his adultery. Similarly, the idea of Estelle duplicating her lover's tattoo is cheapened when we see
Estelle going into the tattooist's, then baring her bosom to
Serafina in the casino (where, incidentally, Williams and
producer Hal Wallis stand around as extras). Even the bawdry of Williams's bananas is lost when we see the bananas
loaded by bundles!

Alvaro suffers the most from this insensitive visualization. We see Alvaro get his tattoo in preparation for his
date with Serafina. He even haggles over the price. In the
play we share Serafina's shock when the muscular clown,
who in so many ways reminds her of her husband, suddenly
reveals a rose tattoo. For a moment we share her hope that a
miracle has happened, that the Madonna has answered her
prayers by sending her a resurrection of Rosario—or a reasonable facsimile. By showing Alvaro's preparation, the film
squanders this moment of mystery and faith, and cheapens
Alvaro's devotion. Moreover, this example suggests that the
director was concerned more with conveying the plot to his
film audience in a clear chronological sequence than with exploring the plot's thematic and emotional registers.

In the same vein, Mann altered the eventual union of
Serafina and Alvaro, completely replacing the element of
passion with comedy. In the play, Serafina and Alvaro ar-

range for his stealthy return to make love to her. The Act III curtain drops at the moment of Serafina's return from the reverential dead to the lusty living. But in the film, Alvaro is drunk and fumbling when he comes back to Serafina. He trips over chickens, wakes up crying children in the neighborhood, is shot at, and passes out on the floor. Serafina draws a curtain over him with motherly affection: "A clown like that with my husband's body." She remains committed to her husband. Mann has reduced the woman's passion to a tolerance of impotence.

This change has further ramifications. In the play, Serafina finally approves Rosa's romance with the sailor once she has felt her own stirrings of lust and life. As the film has not allowed Serafina this passion, she frees Rosa to Jack not out of lively sympathy, but as a cold matchmaker. Secondly, when Rosa finds Alvaro in the play, Serafina's reaction is to lie to her daughter by pleading innocence. In the film, this plea is no lie. The film loses both the heightened tension of the scene in the play, and Williams's point that lying and hypocrisy are a greater danger than the free flow of passionate relationships.

The film dramatizes a radically different ethic than does the play, then. It also has a significantly simpler tone. For the charm of the play lies in its counterpointing the passionate vision of love with the comic. High passion is balanced by a persistent tone of self-parody; the playfulness keeps the operatic tendency in check.

But the comic element predominates in the film. For instance, the neighbor's rampaging goat, a symbol of uncontrollable lust in the play, is domesticated in the screen version. When the goat imperiously appears in close-up to start the last scene, Jack and Rosa have agreed to marry, so metaphorically the goat is under harness. The screenplay omits all reference to the goat's satyr-like powers. Even the scenes of the goat's rampage are played as comedy, with Alvaro pretending to be a matador. This bullfight parody suggests that the goat is no threat to anything; the goat needs the corrida analogy to seem to be a worthy opponent for the trucker. The effect is not "weird and beautiful" (p.94) as Williams's stage directions prescribe, but shallow and ludicrous.

One might perhaps argue that the film must be taken as a kind of shorthand, in which by convention "marriage" means "passion." Certainly the film is true to the play's idea that love leads to community. Thus Serafina's misguided devotion to Rosario isolates her from her neighbors. And she imposes her isolation on Rosa with "You no study civics no more." The film presents Serafina's acceptance of Alvaro as a public, communal act, observed and celebrated by the neighborhood. So in this respect the film is true to an important thrust of the play. And the comic tones that the film gives Alvaro's loving and the goat's wildness have some basis in the playful spirit of the original. What is lacking in the film, though, is the balance between the serious and the light, the passionate and the ironic, the rose and the banana.

So the film may fairly represent the events of the play, but it lacks Williams's challenge to familiar, domestic morality. In this respect, the film actually subverts the play. And it fails to preserve the resonance of Williams's ambiguous vision. This dilution may be due to director Daniel Mann, whose film work was solidly in the tradition of stolid, domestic realism (*Come Back Little Sheba, About Mrs. Leslie, I'll Cry Tomorrow*).[2] Mann was not at ease with Williams's kind of subtleties and irony. After all, Williams would plan a play called "The Poker Night" but he would transform it into *A Streetcar Named Desire*. From a base of realism Williams would spin out poetic drama. But in the filming of *The Rose Tattoo*, the poetic turned to prose.

Then too the adaptation was compromised by the timidity of commercial film making in America in the 1950s. Our discussion of the next Williams film, *Baby Doll*, will help us to appreciate the social pressures behind the domestication of *The Rose Tattoo*. And yet Hollywood was attracted to sensational best sellers. Unfortunately, its bravery in purchasing controversial works rarely extended to the way they were filmed. Hence the Hollywood axiom: good stories about bad girls are made into bad stories about good girls. In its conversion of passion into marriage, *The Rose Tattoo* bears out this saying.

4

Baby Doll

(1956)

Tennessee Williams wrote *Baby Doll* for the screen at the behest of Elia Kazan, with whom he had collaborated so successfully on *A Streetcar Named Desire*. The film was first announced as *The Whip-Hand*, then as *Mississippi Woman*, but it opened as *Baby Doll* in New York on December 18, 1956.

Baby Doll set off a storm. The National Legion of Decency condemned it as "morally repellent both in theme and treatment," for dwelling "almost without variation or relief upon carnal suggestiveness in action, dialogue and costuming." Cardinal Spellman attacked the film from the pulpit of St. Patrick's Cathedral.[1] Several critics defended the film as a moral, realistic work,[2] but it failed commercially, largely due to the pressure that religious groups placed on their congregations and upon theater owners. Today the film seems an innocuous black comedy. Lacking nudity, violence, sexual activity, and even indecorous language, *Baby Doll* could run on family hour television—if anyone would watch it! Even its notorious poster—Carroll Baker in a crib—is mild by current standards.

Williams took most of the plot from his one-act play, *27 Wagons Full of Cotton*. Baby Doll Meighan (Carroll Baker) is a voluptuous blonde in the Deep South, married to Archie Lee Meighan (Karl Malden) but allowed to keep her virginity until she turns 20. The film opens on the eve of that birthday. Archie has lost his cotton gin business to the Syndicate Plantation, owned by a smooth Sicilian immigrant, Vacarro (Eli Wallach). While Vacarro is celebrating his success, Archie burns down the Syndicate gin. Vacarro suspects Archie and so brings him his cotton (27 wagons full) to gin. Sending Archie off to find a replacement part, Vacarro flatters, questions, and tricks Baby Doll into admitting her husband's guilt. Then he playfully chases Baby Doll through the attic. When the floor crumbles at her feet, Vacarro forces her to sign a statement of Archie's guilt. Baby Doll seems disappointed that Vacarro was after her only for her confession. They have a moment of nonsexual intimacy when she watches him nap in her crib. When Archie returns, Vacarro promises to give him more business, which will involve more afternoons with Baby Doll.

Williams also drew plot elements from this one-acter, *The Unsatisfactory Supper*. Baby Doll's Aunt Rose Comfort (Mildred Dunnock) cooks for the Meighans. When Archie returns, he invites Vacarro to supper. But Aunt Rose forgets to cook the greens. Archie takes out his frustrations on Aunt Rose and orders her to leave. Vacarro offers to take her in as his housekeeper.

At the end of the film, Archie is arrested for shooting at Vacarro. Baby Doll and Aunt Rose go back into the house, wondering whether Vacarro will remember to return for them the next day. Williams's published screenplay ends with more certainty, with Archie driven away and Vacarro holding out his arms to catch Baby Doll as she drops, like a ripe fruit, from a tree. As Karl Malden recalls, neither Williams nor Kazan were ever satisfied with the ending they worked out.[3]

Two major themes in the film are dispossession and dislocation. Literally, Archie is dispossessed of his furniture. Figuratively, Vacarro dispossesses him of Baby Doll and Aunt Rose, thereby costing Archie his pride and integrity. And having complained about mortgaging himself to please Baby Doll, Archie must use his wife to win Vacarro's business. On the other hand, Baby Doll is dispossessed of her childhood, her

privacy, and her self-determination by her unromantic marriage to Archie. The theme occurs even in casual conversation: "I wouldn't be putting you out?" Vacarro asks Archie,
with elaborate innocence, when invited to dinner.

Vacarro himself is the primary embodiment of dislocation, an outsider in an unsympathetic land. When his cotton gin burns to the ground, the witnesses gloat at his loss and
the sheriff is slow to help him trace the arsonist. Even at the
end of the film, Archie tries to make a deal with the sheriff
against Vacarro, "one white man to another." With no help
from the community, Vacarro is left to his own honor and his
own resources. Vacarro's Italian energy—both physical and
moral—is thus contrasted to the decaying, impotent WASP
community.

Vacarro's situation as a stranger in a strange land is expanded to betoken the human condition: "people come into
this world without instructions of where to go, what to do, so
they wander a little and then go away." Vacarro at least has
his honor to direct him. But the other white characters have
no such security. Baby Doll is a girl in a woman's situation, so
her very marriage is an emblem of dislocation. Aunt Rose because she is too old and Archie because he is too vain in his
ambitions are both dislocated figures, without security or direction. This theme is visualized during the attic chase, when
the floor crumbles under Baby Doll's feet and she has to
reach out to Vacarro for rescue. Before he will save her,
though, he insists on her signed declaration of the truth, as if
the human connection must be based upon truth. Archie has a
comic version of the anxiety of lost footing: "Baby Doll, if
your Daddy turned in his grave as often as you say he'd turn
in his grave, that old man would plow up the graveyard."

The personal dislocation of the characters is given a social dimension by the poverty and decay of the Meighan plantation. The title graphics contrast the precarious present to
the solid past by setting wicker letters against the classical
columns of the mansion. The Meighan house is falling apart.
So Baby Doll cowers against chipped, peeling pillars as she

flees Vacarro. The first shot of the film is of the decrepit mansion amid skeletal trees. But by the end, the atmosphere has changed to the richly leaved tree in which the maturing Baby Doll and the lively Vacarro hide from Archie.

The tree suggests that nature is a constant, a norm, which the wavering humans might do well to acknowledge. Vacarro stands under the tree when he learns that Baby Doll's marriage has not been consummated. While they hide in its plush foliage, Archie pounds his fist against the dry earth beneath, wailing for Baby Doll. The power of nature is also imaged in the grass that grows through the floorboards of the old Pierce-Arrow in the yard. Man's mobility and style fade away, but nature persists. The verdant car recalls the violets breaking the rocks at the end of *Camino Real*.

Vacarro is portrayed as being in harmony with nature. From the well that the others are not strong enough to tap, Vacarro pumps up cool water for Baby Doll, while a cock crows approvingly in the background. As well, Vacarro seems at ease in the film's hot, bright, summer afternoon, while Archie sweats profusely, even indoors. For in his manner and in his marriage, Archie is out of tune with nature. He is outside the fertility cycle, for he has imposed himself upon an unwilling wife. Confirming Archie's association with sterility, Baby Doll teases him about his bald spot:

> There was an old witch named Granny Crow.
> Wherever she spit, no grass would grow.

Indeed, the last we see of Archie is his bald spot, as he bows his head when the sheriff drives him away. There is also a comic version of Archie's futile attempt to stave off natural forces—Aunt Rose's struggle to keep the hen, Old Fussy, out of the kitchen. The hen, the cocksure Vacarro, and the natural order of truth and vitality, all win out in the end.

The characters who seem closest to nature in the film are the various blacks whom Kazan added as a kind of silent chorus. They accept their own poverty and laugh at the pretenses by which the whites try to conceal their frustrations and shame. The blacks here anticipate the beach boys in *The Night of the Iguana*: they have an elemental directness and charm that contrasts with the deviousness, malice, and affectation of the whites.

Although shot in black and white, the film develops a significant color scheme. It contrasts the bleached-out, sterile world of the whites with the vitality of the blacks. For instance, Archie always wears white on white. Vacarro wears only black, and has prominent black hair and a moustache. As Baby Doll grows from Archie's property to Vacarro's personal friend, her dress changes from white to black. In one typical shot late in the film, Archie stands against a white wall, in a white suit, talking on the phone, but under a threatening, black, triangular shadow. Behind him, Baby Doll's black-sleeved arm reaches to put out the light so she can kiss Vacarro.

Of course, there are shades within white. The white swing around which Vacarro weaves the early stages in his seduction of Baby Doll registers bright white in long shot, but gray in the close-ups, when Vacarro's pressure upon Baby Doll intensifies. The photography of Boris Kaufman brilliantly isolates parts of the swing and modulates the brightness to help Kazan convey delicate changes in mood throughout the scene.

Baby Doll is a remarkable film. The photography[4] and performances are exemplary. Only once is there an obtrusive bit of symbolism: when Archie returns to find his wife and rival together, the three characters position themselves in various formal order along the staircase inside, as if jockeying for a superior place on a ladder of success. But for the most part the film is sensitive and subtle. Seemingly easy effects are found to have multiple meaning. Thus when the black waitress sings "I Shall Not Be Moved," she is expressing not just her own spirit but the stubbornness of the sheriff who ordered her to sing.

Again one is impressed by the combined effort of Kazan and Williams. Individual scenes reveal Kazan's characteristic concerns: the eating scene, where the occasion forces the characters to set aside their animosities; the maturing of the adolescent; the earnest immigrant's success; the water and swing scenes. All these have analogues in Kazan's other work. But the general impact of the drama is Williams's. There is Williams's sense of the cruelty of man (in the fire scene); the need for a fertile outsider (notably, an Italian) to free the stagnant community from its hypocrisy and torpor; and the horror of a marriage that is based upon private humiliation and a public lie. *Baby Doll* is a Williams work in another way, too—it is an extremely funny film. There is horror in the fire scene, fright in the attic chase, sensuality in the posture of Baby Doll, and a stern moral view overall, but the film remains extremely funny. It is Williams's best film comedy.

5

Cat on a Hot Tin Roof
(1958)

The next successful collaboration between Tennessee Williams and Elia Kazan was the stage production of *Cat on a Hot Tin Roof,* which opened on Broadway on March 24, 1955, and won Williams his second Pulitzer Prize. But the direction of the film version was assigned to Richard Brooks, a novelist turned screenwriter-director, who interrupted a career in popular genre films to attempt several challenging adaptations: *The Brothers Karamazov* (1958), *Cat on a Hot Tin Roof* (1958), *Elmer Gantry* (1960), Williams's *Sweet Bird of Youth* (1962), and *Lord Jim* (1964).

Brooks's first Williams film proved a remarkable success at the box-office. *Cat* was the biggest grosser of 1958, the tenth biggest that MGM ever had, and the biggest of all the Williams adaptations. But the critical reception was less kind. Generally, reviewers found the film too mechanical an adaptation.[1] But it seems to me to be a creative, faithful performance of the text with but a single, albeit disastrous, lapse in discretion.

The plot can be paraphrased simply: Maggie strives to get her husband Brick to make love to her again, and to keep her in-laws from cutting her out of her father-in-law's will. But such a summary does not do justice to the depth and significance of Williams's characterization.

For example, Big Daddy Pollitt is a self-made millionaire who is dying of cancer. His family and doctors shield him

38

from that knowledge. Big Daddy wants to leave his empire to his favorite son Brick but is worried about Brick's alcoholism, the breakdown of Brick's relations with Maggie, and their failure to have a child. So Big Daddy may have to leave his wealth to his older son Gooper, an oily lawyer with a shrike for a wife (Mae) and a brood of "no-neck monsters" for children.

Then there is Brick, a faded star athlete sunk in cynicism and despair since the suicide of his best friend Skipper. Skipper loved Brick, but both men were so conditioned by their fear of homosexuality that they could not admit their love for each other. Skipper and Maggie made love once because, as Maggie recalls, "it made us both feel a little bit closer to [Brick]" (p.133). Because Brick's fastidious idealism denied them the full expression of their love for him, they "made love to each other to dream it was you" (p.133). When Skipper phoned Brick to bring his feelings into the open, Brick rejected Skipper's confession of love. Skipper then killed himself. Now Brick charges that Skipper committed suicide because Maggie seduced him: Brick therefore refuses to sleep with Maggie. Finally Big Daddy forces Brick to recognize his guilt; in return, Brick lashes back with the truth about his father's cancer.

Maggie is the nervous, highly charged cat on a hot tin roof—passionate, frustrated, and tortured, but unwilling to jump off. Because she fears poverty and loves Brick and Big Daddy, at the end of the play she announces that she is carrying Brick's baby. Admiring Maggie's spirit, Brick supports her lie. Privately, Maggie threatens to withhold Brick's liquor until he has impregnated her.

The play lends itself to filming because it was conceived in a more realistic mode than, say, *The Glass Menagerie* and *Summer and Smoke*. It seems a kind of afterthought when Williams, at the end of his "Notes for the Designer" (p.106), suggests that the interior walls of the set dissolve mysteriously into air, with a starry sky above the rooms. The play is above all realistic. The large, amusing, and well-developed cast of characters further facilitates the filming. It is also one of the reasons that Williams often cites *Cat* as the favorite of his plays; others are Big Daddy's crude eloquence and the play's concern with the most important theme in Williams's work: "the mendacity that underlies the thinking and feeling of our affluent society." [2]

Certainly mendacity is the main concern of the play—and of most of the film. In an early addition in the film, Maggie warns Brick that "There are some things in this world you've got to face," but the characters avoid painful truths and lie to others and to themselves. Thus Brick blames his disintegration on the mendacity of all around him. But even here Brick lies to himself, by failing to recognize the guilt he feels for Skipper's death. Brick prefers to blame Maggie. Then too the entire family lies to preserve Big Daddy's spirit in the face of his cancer. Time and again, the characters turn on music, a false smile or laugh, a euphemism, or silence, to ignore or to deny an unappealing truth. When Maggie lies about her pregnancy, her mendacity is tempered by her liveliness. "Truth, truth," Brooks has her declaim, "Everyone keeps hollerin' about the truth. But the truth is as dirty as lies." When Brick supports her lie ("truth is something desperate, an' she's got it" [p.222]), he senses that her lie is a promise. For Maggie is prepared to work to make her lie come true.

A related theme is lack of privacy. Literally, Maggie and Big Daddy are continually bothered by the eavesdropping of Gooper and Mae, and by the noisy interruptions of their rude children. Williams uses this lack of privacy as a metaphor for the shame and self-consciousness by which one's development is restricted by public pressure. The most touching example is Skipper's love for Brick, which was doomed by Brick's attitude toward the homosexuals who had owned the plantation before Big Daddy. Even Skipper's friendship with Brick was soured by Brick's fear of public opprobrium. Typical of Williams, the sympathetic characters are the weak, sensitive, and vulnerable ones, while the villains, the vulgar, the monsters, are the most secure. As Maggie remarks, with understandable rue, the no-neck monsters have no necks to wring. The character with the longest, most beautiful neck,[3] Maggie, has the most awareness, the most to win, the most to lose, and she suffers most from the spying and the judgments of the others.

The sexual terms in which Williams presents these themes were clearly a problem for the film adapter. But considering that the movie was released within two years of the furor over *Baby Doll*, the film is remarkably frank. At times the film is even freer than the play: Big Daddy's "makes me sick" becomes "makes me puke." More often, however, the language is subdued, as when Big Daddy's "Crap" is changed to "Bull" and his salty stories are toned down or omitted. In the film, Maggie claims that she left Skipper after only a kiss ("Nothing happened"). Nevertheless, the ads stressed the film's sexual concerns ("When a marriage goes on the rocks—the rocks are there, right in that bed!").

Of course, American film decorum is not restricted to sex. For example, the references to "cancer" are excised from the text. Voices trail off at the approach of the dread term. Such pussyfooting seems especially inappropriate for this play, since escapist silence and euphemism are varieties of the mendacity under study. For decorum, too, the film softens Williams's religious satire. For instance, the greedy Reverend Tooker, who is angling for a monumental contribution to his church, is changed to a layman exploiting his church affiliation to advance his political career. Brooks further omits Big Daddy's memory of fat priests amid starving children in Barcelona. But Brooks does include at least one religious irony in the film. When Brick confronts the doctor with the mendacity of the family's celebration ("What kind of truth is that?"), we hear the children outside singing "Jesus wants me for a sunbeam." This hymn is sung by "monsters" in a situation of hypocrisy. The line is a euphemism for death (and for the parallel parting remark of the film's doctor: "Sometimes I wish I had a pill to make people disappear"). Perhaps Brooks wanted to acknowledge the bleak representation of religion in the play, without becoming offensive. In any case, the promise of permissiveness was an important factor in the commercial success of the film.

Casting was another. Elizabeth Taylor replaced Barbara Bel Geddes as Maggie the Cat and Paul Newman replaced Ben Gazzara as Brick. Jack Carson's Gooper grew out of his series of roles as the false friend and crook (most notably in the 1954 *A Star Is Born*). From Kazan's original cast, Brooks kept only Burl Ives as Big Daddy and Madeleine Sherwood as Mae.

But these castings were valid for aesthetic considerations. Elizabeth Taylor, for instance, brought to Maggie a hardness, a sexual experience and a nervousness that have not appeared in Bel Geddes's screen work; Bel Geddes tends to be associated with cuddly domesticity (*Panic in the Streets, Fourteen Hours, Vertigo*). Brooks exploits Taylor's legendary beauty, too. He focuses on her legs when she changes her stockings, hoping to arouse Brick. Here Taylor's appeal heightens the force of Brick's withdrawal. In Newman's case, Brooks recalls that he cast the handsome young actor because he could be photographed for long periods of silent thought.[4] His blue eyes are lively in contemplation during most of the first half of the film, when his dialogue is minimal. As it happens, Williams ascribed to Brick "the charm of that cool air of detachment that people have who have given up the struggle," yet still suggesting that a deep level of disturbance persists (p.111), a quality that Newman's eyes express eloquently in the film.

Brooks followed Williams's directions in other respects. For instance, Maggie's big bed remains prominent behind or between her husband and herself, as Williams recommends (p.105). When Maggie compliments Brick on his continuing attractiveness, she circles the bed with feline invitation and caresses the bedposts. In the last shot of the film, the bed is restored to its proper place in the relationship, the foreground, and Brick throws the pillow onto it, intending to bring Maggie after. True, in the play it is Maggie who takes the initiative and throws the pillow, but the film's change is an extension of Brick's willingness to support Maggie in her lie. Brooks makes more explicit the reconciliation that the stage production implied at the end of the third act (Williams's original third act was more pessimistic than the version worked out with Kazan).[5]

Brooks's treatment of Brick's sexuality is also true to Williams. The film reviewers concluded that Brick was a homosexual, largely because he would wipe away a kiss from Liz Taylor, one suspects! One reviewer declared that "Brick is the best dramatised study of homosexuality I have seen."[6] But another critic contends that Brooks "played down the deviation motif."[7] Williams himself has remarked that Brick is not a homosexual, but that his self-disgust derives from his having lived so long with lies.[8] This is clear enough from the play. For one thing, Maggie tells Brick that his platonic relationship with Skipper was innocent and "couldn't be anything else, you being you" (p.134). So there was not much homosexuality to be "played down" in the movie; there was only public suspicion about Brick's friendship with Skipper.

Brooks retains Brick's defense of the innocence of that friendship. Moreover, he defines Brick's sexual problem in three specific scenes. First, in the introductory scene between Brick and Maggie, Brooks has Brick wield his crutch in a series of phallic positions that imply that he has a sexual disability, rather than a deviance. Second, Brooks adds a shot of Brick in the bathroom, burying his face in Maggie's slip and caressing it in agony. This clearly suggests that Brick still desires his wife. Third, Brick's heterosexuality is confirmed by some precise parallels with his father, who at 65 and near death still has a lecherous eye and ambition. Even as Brick recoils from Maggie's touch, refuses to drink from her glass, and wipes away her kiss, Brooks has Big Daddy turn and walk away from Big Mama's offer of a birthday kiss. Thus we see that both men have strong sexual appetites for women, for all their aversion toward their wives.

This parallel in the men's behavior replaces a verbal parallel in the text, where both men remark wryly, "Wouldn't it be funny if /it/ was true" that their wives sincerely loved them through their years of unhappiness together. Brooks often omits a formal or a self-conscious line from the play, because the realistic setting of a film does not allow the kind of artificial statements that work on stage. So, too, Brooks trusts the energy of Taylor's performance and omits Maggie's line, "My hat is still in the ring, and I am determined to win." Maggie in general seems less garrulous in the film than in the play, because Brooks often shows us the incidents that Maggie otherwise had to describe to Brick. Thus we enjoy the grim sketch of Big Daddy's domestic afflictions at his airport reception and his birthday supper. In the film we see what in the play Maggie described.

To visualize the atmosphere that Big Daddy finds in his house, an atmosphere reeking of mendacity, Brooks shoots the other family members in extremely formal arrangement. From the moment Big Daddy learns he is dying and calls his family liars, the other Pollitts are shown together in neat, formal ordering, as if in a theatrical blocking. In an earlier shot, Maggie plays solitaire in the foreground, Mae fusses with a child behind her, Big Mama talks on the phone, and Gooper eavesdrops on Big Daddy's conversation with Brick. The shot shows the pockets of isolation and self-concern in the family, despite their pretense of togetherness. Moreover, the shot appears just as Big Daddy is telling Brick of the mendacity he has had to live with all his life. In all these shots, the theatrical arrangement of the characters conveys the falseness of the situation; the archness in the image undercuts the characters' familial pose.

The outdoor sequences that Brooks added are as sensitive as this interior pattern. He begins before the credits with a sequence in which we see Brick break his leg while drunkenly trying to run the hurdles in the empty stadium where he had known his athletic glory. In addition to showing what the play only described, Brooks has us hear the crowd's roaring that Brick imagines (or remembers). Because we share

Brick's illusion and experience, we enter the fiction with him as our figure of identification. This is a necessary counter-weight to the stronger drawing force of the Taylor image (in 1958). Finally, the scene is an early demonstration of the power of fantasy—and the greater weakness of the flesh. By "hearing" the nonexistent crowd, we learn how difficult it can be to distinguish truth from falseness, especially when it is the false that we crave.

Two other outdoor scenes are used to express the expansive spirit of Big Daddy. In the first, he has his fields and racehorses behind him as he tells Maggie, "I'm gonna live ... I got so many feelings in me and I'm gonna use them all." This scene does not occur in the play, but it demonstrates what Maggie told Brick, that Big Daddy prefers them over Mae and Gooper. Moreover, it helps to present Big Daddy as the most powerful figure in the play (with the possible exception of Maggie), the only one who lives and talks heedless of others' regard. Big Daddy needs open-air scenes to suggest his energy and power, and, of course, the scene sets up a dramatic contrast to the dingy basement to which Big Daddy retreats when he learns that he is dying.

Big Daddy's other outdoor scene is the turning point in the film. Here Brick and Big Daddy work through to expose each other's secret: Brick's guilt about Skipper's death and Big Daddy's cancer. The conversation begins with Brick on his sofa; but Big Daddy's pursuit of the truth drives Brick off the couch, out of the room, into the rain, and into an open con-vertible. These are images of increasing exposure, as the truth emerges. The rain works as an image of the truth to which the characters are exposing themselves. Thus, it is her-alded by ominous claps of thunder. Then, too, the truth is—like the rain—an uncontrollable power which cannot be turned back once its force has been unleashed. Again like the rain, the truth is inescapable, except for the temporary shel-ter in the house that reeks of mendacity. Finally, as Big Daddy stands there, letting the truth of his cancer seep in, there is a long moment of quiet peace. The rain runs down his face like

tears; man and nature are at one, in the truth. There is also a
difference in how the men react to the rain. Big Daddy exposes himself, removing his jacket to drape it over his son.
But Brick, ever the weaker, tries to escape. And in a brilliant
image of moral paralysis and emotional blockage, Brick's car
spins its wheels deeper and deeper into the mud. Here, as in
the previous example, the film's new setting provides apt
metaphors for the themes of the scene.

So far we have considered the successes in Brooks's adaptation. However, I did suggest that a single indiscretion se-
verely damages this film as a representation of Williams's
play. This error occurs because Brooks moved and expanded
the two pages where Big Daddy tells Brick about his ac-
quisitive visit to Europe—"A great big auction, that's all it is,
that bunch of worn-out old places." In the play, this exchange
occurs near the beginning of the long, intense conversation
that ends with the exposure of the truth. But in the film, it occurs in the basement where Big Daddy goes to consider his
dying.

The new scene works dramatically in the film. Brooks
cuts between the men in the dark basement and the brightly
lit living room, where Gooper and Mae attempt to win Big
Mama's cooperation in disinheriting Brick. This juxtaposition
contrasts the following: the living room lies with the basement
honesty; Mae's hatred with Brick's love; Gooper's power
with Brick's (emotional) and Big Daddy's (physical) debility.
Further, the greed of the plotters is undercut by the fact that
Big Daddy now finds no solace in his pile of possessions.

But the scene violates the thematic proportions of the
play. In the first place, in the original it represented a digres-
sion in Big Daddy's chat with Brick, one of the tendencies that
make it "so damn hard for people to talk" (p.151). But in the
film, the same comments work to draw the men together after
the shock of Brick's disclosure outside. Similarly, in the play
Big Daddy moved quickly through these thoughts on property,
Brick dismissed them, and they progressed to more important
concerns. But in the film, the men move from the more

serious topics to this one. The effect is to suggest that materialism is a more serious concern than mendacity and its obverse, the courage to face life and death directly.

The scene also admits an unfortunate element of sentimentality, which softens Williams's vision in the same way his characters' euphemisms do. The film's Big Daddy tries to ease his death by surveying his goods. An old suitcase reminds him of his own father, a tramp who gave him nothing—nothing but time, love, and happy memories. Brooks also encumbers Brick with an embarrassing array of irrelevant platitudes, to wit: wealth is not as important as family love. And happy memories are one's richest legacy. And Brick didn't want a boss, he wanted love. So Brick here becomes the victim of an unloving father while in the play his problem was that he could not handle all the love people had for him (his father, mother, Maggie, Skipper). It is almost as if Brooks feared that his audience would not understand Williams's point in the drama, and so instead he tossed in a number of familiar lessons that they could handle.

Perhaps that is why Brooks also includes a parallel to *Citizen Kane*, in his awed pan across a landscape of possessions, memories fossilized, that suggets a powerful man untouched by his empire. When Brick pauses to spin his tricycle wheel, one half expects to read "Rosebud" on the handlebar. As with the homilies, Brooks here reduces the play to a more familiar form. The unique Big Daddy is reduced to a stock figure in the Kane tradition. As a consequence, the play is converted into an attack on materialism. Both by the arrangement of the original scenes and in his addition of new, but familiar, material, Brooks has emphasized the folly of materialistic greed over Williams's theme: mendacity in the human condition.

Brooks's additions betray the play in the very way that Williams had warned against in his stage directions. Williams intended to catch "that cloudy, flickering, evanescent—fiercely charged—interplay of live human beings in the thundercloud of a common crisis," but still to leave some mystery in the revelation of character. Williams warned against "'pat' conclusions, facile definitions which make a play just a play, not a snare for the truth of human experience" (pp.167-68), but the pat conclusion is the very snare into which Brooks fell.

The basement scene in the film can be explained—if not excused—as a critical observation Brooks is making on the play. The intimacy that the film reestablishes between father and son, and the specific terms of their new understanding, may be Brooks's suggestion that Williams wrote *Cat on a Hot Tin Roof* in order to reconcile himself in his mind with his own father.[9] Perhaps the play did grow out of Williams's family experience, but its meaning and effect are far greater than mere personal reflection would be. Of couse, all performances of a play are interpretations—critical observations about the text. But Brooks forces his reading on the film, in too important a spot and at too great a length. Brooks's idea may be correct, but he puts it forth in a way that seriously distorts the original work.

In any case, Williams had objected that the film lacked "the purity of the play. It was jazzed up, hoked up a bit."[10] And elsewhere: it was "somehow, not quite what I meant to say."[11] But for the bulk of the film, Brooks delivers Williams's meaning very well. Only in the basement scene does his reading impinge upon the original; that it comes so late in the film may hinder our just estimation of the remainder.

Curiously, Brooks is quoted in the studio pressbook for the film as claiming complete fidelity to the stage version: "Any substitution that would make this play ordinary or that would change its mainspring would be criminal." But Brooks's infusion of homilies and his misrepresentation of the tension between Brick and Big Daddy—these two additions of the "ordinary"—do damage the adaptation. "Criminal" may be too harsh a word, though. "Delinquent" may be better. "Criminal" should be saved for Brooks's 1962 adaptation of *Sweet Bird of Youth*.

6

Suddenly Last Summer
(1959)

There were three problems to overcome in filming *Suddenly Last Summer*. First, there was the familiar issue of toning down the sensational elements of a drama to appease the more conservative film audience. Yet, a scant three years after the innocent *Baby Doll* was abused, the public accepted this Tennessee Williams play with its suggestions of homosexuality, nymphomania, rape, cannibalism, voyeurism, and a pinch of prefrontal lobotomy. The Legion of Decency declined to condemn the film, citing its obvious moral purpose. Clearly the climate had changed since Williams first ventured into the cinema with his mature work.

The second problem involved the allegorical, non-realistic nature of the original play. The extremities of Williams's subject matter were tempered here by the air of unreality created by several special effects in the stage presentation—savage beasts heard in the mansion garden, wild birds heard behind a character's speech, and fade-outs in the lighting. The danger in filming the play was that this element of fantasy in the stage presentation might be lost. In Williams's view, the film failed by turning the allegorical drama "into a literal film, which made it absolutely unbelievable ... and rather distasteful." He "loathed" the film.[1]

The third problem was more unusual. The feature-length film was based upon a one-act play, so that some expansion was necessary. Moreover, the play was originally performed with another one-acter, "Something Unspoken," which opened under the collective title *Garden District* in New York on January 7, 1958. The first play was quieter and more realistic, as if to prepare the audience for the shock of *Suddenly Last Summer*. The plays were suitable companion pieces, for both depict the vanity of a class, through the characters of Cornelia Scott and Violet Venable, respectively. Then, too, in both plays the senior woman loses her power to a younger one. In both plays there is an attempt to suppress a secret; silence is a weapon in both. *Suddenly Last Summer* gained a realistic base and the aforementioned points of emphasis in performance by occurring in the context of the other play. But the film was the one play, self-contained, so a true adaptation would have to compensate for the loss of the companion play. This director Joseph Mankiewicz and scriptwriter Gore Vidal did by amplifying the social dimension, increasing the interior life of the characters, and elaborating upon Williams's expressive setting to convey the sense of the "garden district." As a result, the film may at times seem an extremely free adaptation, but the themes and mood of the play are conveyed faithfully.

In the play, Violet Venable promises a sizable donation to a struggling mental hospital if its surgeon, Dr. Cukrowicz, will lobotomize her niece Catherine. Mrs. Venable seeks to erase what she maintains is an obscene fantasy from Catherine's mind: that Mrs. Venable's poet son, Sebastian, had used Catherine (and earlier, his mother) to attract homosexual lovers, and that he was cannibalized by a gang of boys in the heat of summer in Amalfi.

The plot develops several of Williams's major themes. Foremost is the characters' refusal to admit any vision of reality but their own. Moreover, Mrs. Venable would go to cruel lengths to avoid any alternative vision of her son. Catherine maintains her sanity by clinging to her own vision in the face of her aunt's pressure and desertion by her mother and brother.

Williams's second major theme is the need for balance in one's vision of life, the need for a whole vision that will embrace both the beauty and the horror of creation. Thus Sebastian is destroyed for resigning himself to a partial vision. His God is the terror of a sky filled with devouring birds that gorge themselves on the underbellies of baby sea turtles. As Sebastian commits himself to this cruel and narrow vision, he too becomes a consumer of flesh. "Blonds were next on the menu," Catherine recalls of that fateful summer, "All summer long Sebastian was famished for blonds." And she accuses Violet: "You fed on life, both of you." The images of eating place Violet and Sebastian in the spirit of the devouring birds. Hence the poetic justice in Sebastian's death; he is eaten by the youths he has, in his fashion, fed upon. Consistent with the fact that Sebastian's concept of life is incomplete, we see only pieces of him in the film—down from the waist, his back, finally just his lifted, wilting hand. In the play he is not seen at all. But his appearance in the film is more sensitive than Rosario's was in *The Rose Tatoo;* it depicts his fragmentary being.

Williams's third theme is his dread of a sterilized, uniform humanity. The horror of *Suddenly Last Summer* is not in the grisly tale Catherine tells, but in the plan to operate on Catherine's brain to remove an unattractive story, whether it be the truth or a fantasy. The film emphasizes Williams's faith in the unusual quirks of mankind. When Dr. Cukrowicz has Cathy put in the nurses' ward of the asylum instead of in the patients', his superior remarks "This is very unorthodox." "So is insanity," replies Cukrowicz. "That's why we're here." The human view is that man must be different, distinctive. The Lion's View (the name of the asylum) is that differences between individuals are to be eradicated, even if this involves cutting out pieces of the brain. The film itself opens with a subtle deviance. The credits appear against a dark brick wall. A sign pointing right directs the viewer to the asylum entrance, but the camera brings us inside by panning left instead. The camera gently aligns us with the deviant, by moving us against the command of the sign.

Williams's fourth theme is a paradoxical corollary of the third theme. If man is an unruly creature, with an uncontrollable imagination, his wildness is still preferable to the savagery beneath the veneer of civilization. For even the most seemingly "civilized" can be found to be savage. The best example is the cruelty and selfishness of the most elegant, most civilized character in the drama, Violet Venable. To preserve her illusions she would have her niece's mind ruined. Williams imaged forth the savagery of Violet Venable in the overgrown, thick wilderness that Sebastian called his garden.

The film elaborates upon the wilderness image. For example, our first impression of the Venable mansion is its huge, white colonial pillars—emblematic of Southern grace and elegance—but with the savage garden inside. Normally a garden is a symbol of man's harmony with and control over the forces of nature. Like a gentle gardener, Cukrowicz detaches himself from the principle of savagery: "Nature is not created in the image of man's compassion," he admits, but he practices a humane alternative. However, Violet and Sebastian abandon themselves to the morality of the jungle. Oliver Messel's design for the garden in the film eschews the Dali-like, fleshy pulps that Williams prescribed, but is more frightening in its seeming realism. (The part of Violet's Venus's-fly-trap—"a devouring organism aptly named for the Goddess of Love"—is played by a remodeled pitcher plant, as the true Venus's-flytrap looked too innocent!). [2]

Moreover, Mankiewicz extends the garden imagery beyond the mansion. For example, when Violet visits Catherine in the asylum, Catherine has a flower picture over her bed while behind Violet is a steaming smokestack. The moral and aesthetic values here rest with Catherine. Again, the asylum sunroom where Cukrowicz entertains Violet, a few potted plants and some flowered upholstery are ambivalent images of nature controlled. In their lack of vitality they represent what Violet would have Catherine become. Yet in their warmth and charm they suggest a comforting nature that is antithetical to the violence and savagery of the Venable garden.

Mankiewicz introduces the theme of civilized savagery in the second scene of the film, when Cukrowicz performs psychosurgery. As he makes his opening incision, a banister breaks in the viewing balcony above him. Then the light flickers and goes out. Cukrowicz makes a short, bitter speech about "the primitive conditions" and leaves. Thus Mankiewicz locates the marvels of modern science in a "primitive" situation. Further, the crumbling banister and flickering light, while they dramatize the clinic's need for Venable funds, are also metaphors for the fragility of the human mind.

Mankiewicz adds to the play in three ways. First, he shows the mental wards to which Catherine would be consigned. This intensifies the horror of her danger. Thus the opening scene begins with a pan across the vacant faces in the women's ward, coming to rest on one woman who is fondling her rag doll. When this woman reappears, having undergone the operation planned for Catherine, she is a pathetic shell, bereft of her doll. Twice Catherine wanders into the wards, both times fleeing unsympathetic treatment from staff or family. These scenes, like the first one, provide a glimpse of Catherine's threatened future, but they also dramatize Williams's major theme, the madness of trying to flee from reality.

Secondly, Mankiewicz expands the tensions involving Dr. Cukrowicz. He extends the character both ethically and romantically. In the play, the doctor is a quiet, cerebral sort, blond and "glacially brilliant." His name is Polish for "sugar," we are told. Williams tends to give Polish names to his characters of untypically Anglo-Saxon vigor—Kowalski—and Italian names to characters of untypically Anglo-Saxon sensuality—Vacarro, Delle Rose. Cukrowicz is one of Williams's most positive characters because he combines science with moral vigor. Mankiewicz emphasizes these qualities in four ways.

First, Cukrowicz's character was deepened by the casting of Montgomery Clift, whose slight build and nervous manner cast him as hypersensitive characters in such films as *From Here to Eternity*, *The Young Lions*, *Judgment at Nuremberg*, and *Lonelyhearts*. Usually Clift plays the patient, not the doctor, even when he assumes the title role of the self-exploring *Freud*. Mankiewicz emphasizes the doctor's humility by framing him in high-angle shots (shooting down on him), particularly in contrast to the low-angle shots of the domineering Violet Venable (Katherine Hepburn). The other alterations confirm that Clift's Cukrowicz is more sensitive than the doctor in the play.

Second, the film Cukrowicz is more intense in his conscience. Rather than glacial brilliance, he possesses warm sympathy: "I'm afraid I'd make a miserable jester," he tells Violet, "You see, I get concerned when people stop wanting to cry." He is also more intense in his reply to Violet's remark that "Sebastian saw the face of God." In the film Cukrowicz fairly leaps in his reply: "I'd like to hear about that." In the play he coolly replies that "doctors look for God, too" (p.33). The response in the film is more intense and more personal. When Catherine calls him Dr. Sugar, then, she is translating both his name and his nature, although it may seem to confirm the diagnosis that she is a dangerous flirt.

Mankiewicz's third extension of Cukrowicz's character is the development of a romance with Catherine. This may bother the conservative critic the most about this adaptation, for it seems to be a box-office concession to the casting of Elizabeth Taylor. But the romance is highly functional. It serves the basic themes of the play, as we shall see.

Cukrowicz's romance with Catherine contrasts with her desertion by her own family. Catherine's mother may speak affectionately of her—"My little girl was always a perfect lamb"—but she leaves Catherine to be sacrificed. Later, when Catherine prepares for her climactic revelation, she throws herself at the doctor passionately: "Hold me. I've been so lonely. Let me, let me," and she kisses him hungrily. When they step out together onto the patio, their unity as a couple contrasts with the insularity of the rest of the family, each member seated behind his own little table. The fugitive emotion between Catherine and Cukrowicz is an antidote to the selfish insularity of the others.

Their romance also suggests a fertility that contrasts with the sterile narcissism of Violet Venable. This difference can even be heard in the sound of their names; the alliteration of "Catherine" and "Cukrowicz" tends to link them, in contrast with the self-containment of Violet Venable. Moreover, Man- kiewicz emphasizes Violet's possessiveness: "Violet and Se- bastian, Sebastian and Violet, that's the way it's always been and always will be. We're lucky to have one another and need no one else." Similarly, when Violet speaks of Sebastian's being "chaste" and jokes about having assisted at the delivery of his annual poem after a nine-month gestation, she is wear- ing a white coat styled like a maternity gown; this suggests that Violet pretends to be a creative force in her son's work. But Violet's relationship to Sebastian is selfish, narcissistic and vain, particularly in contrast to the love that develops be- tween Cukrowicz and Catherine. For beside the greed of Catherine's family and the possessiveness of Violet Venable, the "box-office concession" of the love story comes as a moral corrective and as a breath of fresh air. When the film closes with a shot of the lovers embracing in the garden, their love has turned Sebastian's savage wilderness positively Edenic.

The fourth extension of Cukrowicz's character is the elaboration upon his ethical dilemma. In the play, Cukrowicz is the only doctor. In the film he has a superior, the seedy, pragmatic administrator Dr. Hockstader. Hockstader has a vi- sion that blurs his sense. When he looks out on the vacant lot where his new clinic will stand, he sees his future dream, and dismisses Cukrowicz's realistic view of the rubble as "the past you're looking at." Again, Cukrowicz's romantic involvement with his patient is an attractive alternative to Hock-stader's willingness to sacrifice Catherine for the benefit of his clinic. The addition of the Hockstader character also gives the film a social context, the dimension that the play original-ly drew from *Something Happened*. For Cukrowicz is now torn between his intuition about Catherine and his profes-sional responsibility toward Hockstader. The professional tension provides a minor level of concern, a social issue, that supports the more abstract concerns of the major characters. Hockstader represents one role in Cukrowicz's professional conflict, Catherine the other. In addition, Hockstader's values provide a familiar theme and moral ("What price progress?") for those unwilling to grapple with the major concerns of the work, but without the radical disruptiveness of Richard Brooks's addition to *Cat on a Hot Tin Roof*.

Mankiewicz's final addition involves the film's con-clusion, beginning with Catherine's long, powerful speech, in which she digs out the memory or fantasy that the others have been trying to suppress. This scene is the emotional crux of the drama. But to film it without some technical inflection would have resulted in a deadly, long monologue. Man-kiewicz handled the sequence well.

Catherine begins to tell her story in close-up. There is the old reaction shot, usually of Violet with a double-edged inter-jection ("How he must have loathed being touched by her"). With the mention of the transparent bathing suit that Sebas-tian made her wear, Catherine's memory grows more defi-nite, more physical, and a series of flashbacks begin. Man-kiewicz begins to show what in the play Catherine described. After a few faint double exposures, the images of the past grow as clear as Catherine herself. As she struggles to keep her balance between past and present, or between fantasy and reality, Mankiewicz introduces a split screen. Catherine remains in present focus in a cameo in the lower right corner, while her story fills the screen. This double-tense is charac-teristic of Mankiewicz's narrative style, for he likes the way flashbacks summon up "not only the effect of the past upon the present, but also the degree to which the past *exists* in the present."[3]

Inside Catherine's cameo there are several jump cuts. This is not because Taylor could not give a continuous performance of this arduous scene,[4] but because the jump cuts express the character's tension as the story trickles forth. They suggest the collection of energy and reassertion of will that are necessary for Catherine to recover and release her vision.

For the climax, the past image is itself doubled, the characters appearing as if with ghosts or auras around them. This is one of three violations of the realism in Catherine's "vision." Another is the appearance in Amalfi of a statue seen earlier in Sebastian's jungle-garden—a winged skeleton. Violet and Cukrowicz passed it as she related "the horrible, the inescapable cruelty" of Sebastian's vision of God. The statue's reappearance in Amalfi confirms its inescapability and attributes Sebastian's fate to his espousal of the violent concept of God. In Catherine's flashback, the statue appears when she says that the streets down which Sebastian fled the boys led "nowhere." Too symbolic for the Amalfi landscape, the statue is a poetic link between Sebastian's past and his doom. The third violation of realism occurs when Sebastian runs past a black-dressed skeleton on the ground. Catherine passes it, stops to look again, and finds it to be an ordinary old woman in black. The sequence is shot as a reverse pan, without a cut, so that Sebastian's experience and Catherine's are continuous. Characteristically, Catherine sees normal life where Sebastian perceives images of death and destruction. But the real and the fantastic occupy the same physical space.

Catherine's story is realistic and the intensity of her delivery persuasive. But Mankiewicz has shaded it with just enough surrealism to allow for the possibility that Catherine is relating a fantasy, not a memory. This coheres with the play, where we only hear Catherine's story and her victory is the doctor's admission that "we ought at least to consider the possibility that the girl's story could be true" (p.72). The story need not be the truth for Catherine to be spared the insentience of the lobotomy. These surrealistic touches enabled Mankiewicz to show the events of Catherine's story without making them seem definitely to have occurred. As he has declared, Mankiewicz was attracted to Williams's play by its

> strange mixture of poetry, drama and analytic free-association. It isn't real, it isn't unreal. It doesn't happen but it doesn't not happen.[5]

Mankiewicz's filmic liberties, at this key point preserved the irreality of the drama.

Mankiewicz went slightly beyond Williams's conclusion. In the play Mrs. Venable is furious at Catherine's disclosure, but in the film she finds a surprising peace. When Catherine finishes, Mrs. Venable closes the empty book in which Sebastian was to have written his poem that fateful summer. Her gnarled, old hands caress the clean, white cover. She smiles—as if Sebastian's poem has been completed, or as if Catherine's story has replaced Sebastian's poem. Unable to withstand the shock of Catherine's story, Mrs. Venable has gone mad. In her private elevator, she ascends to the peace of her mad delusion. Again, the film rounds off a moment of the play with expressive action. The uncertainty upon which the play ended is replaced by an ambivalent attitude toward the savage but pathetic Violet Venable. This may be a substitution of emotion for intellect, but it is true to the play.

The film has the most quotable of screenplays, brilliant performances, and some film technique that is at once inventive and responsive to its source. It seems to me to be one of the best "free" adaptations of modern drama that we have on film. Nor would any new production gain from the current permissiveness; the controversial subject matter was handled with suggestive discretion.

Producer Sam Spiegel released an intelligent statement about the film in the pressbook (presumably to arm exhibitors against irate viewers):

What interested me thematically in *Suddenly Last Summer* was delving and prying into the essence of corruption and depravity and bringing out the moral theme that one cannot abuse other human beings without paying for it either with one's life or sanity....

Unfortunately, the same sensitivity did not pervade the studio's publicity department. It lauded the title for its "variety of showmanship uses" and suggested such promotions as these:

—write-in contests around the theme: "Suddenly Last Summer, the most romantic (exciting, fearful, dramatic, etc.) incident happened to me...."

—bank and insurance promotions keyed to fire, theft or other financial disasters which may have occurred "Suddenly Last Summer."

—travel and related tie-ins, e.g., "Suddenly Last Summer, My Front Tire Blew Out (My Headlights Failed...."

That such a fine and serious film could survive the puerilities of the industry speaks well for Spiegel, Joseph Mankiewicz, and Gore Vidal, and for the power of Tennessee Williams's original play.

7

The Fugitive Kind
(1960)

The work over which Tennessee Williams labored the longest must be his 1940 play *Battle of Angels*. Williams began to rewrite it after its first performance. He presented the same material as *Orpheus Descending* in 1957. Two years later Williams refashioned that version—working with screenwriter Meade Roberts—for Sidney Lumet's *The Fugitive Kind*. In many ways, the film is the best version of the basic material.

Williams's play deals with the effects that a roving guitarist in a snakeskin jacket has on a Southern town. The film casts Marlon Brando as the vagabond Val (for Valentine) Xavier (as if Savior), a figure of love and salvation. Xavier attempts to abandon a life of carousing and irresponsibility, but his reform is complicated by three women in the town.

One is Vee Talbott (Maureen Stapleton), the sheriff's wife. She is a kind, generous woman who paints inspired, primitive visions and is frustrated by life with her callous husband and the snoopy town gossips. A second is Carol Cutrere (Joanne Woodward), a disillusioned idealist who tries to keep Val in the life of "jookin'," cruising from one drunken party to the next. The third woman is Lady Torrance (Anna Magnani), a passionate Italian who suffers as the wife of the dying general store owner, Jabe (Victor Jory).

Once Lady's father ran a popular wine-garden outside town. Lady had a passionate love affair with Carol's brother, David (John Baragrey). She was carrying his child when he left her for a more profitable marriage to another woman. At the same time, Lady's father was caught selling wine to the Negroes. On this pretext, local vigilantes burned down the arbor, and Lady's father in it. With Jabe apparently dying now, Lady hires Val to clerk in her store, behind which she plans to open a confectionery modelled after her father's arbor. Eventually, she falls in love with Val and conceives his child. But the malevolent Jabe grows jealous. He gloats about having helped burn Lady's father. Then he sets fire to the confectionery and blames Val. Lady dies protecting Val from Jabe's gunfire.

The town first turns against Val because of his friendship with the outcast Carol. He is ordered to leave when Sheriff Talbott catches him (innocently) holding Mrs. Talbott. Finally, Val is prevented from safely departing by Lady's announcement of her pregnancy and her refusal to leave with him until she has spited Jabe's malice by opening her dreamed-of confectionery. Thus the women, who most benefit from the love and the power of the vagabond, prevent both his safe stay and his departure.

The film differs from *Orpheus Descending* in two basic ways. First, the element of allegorical abstraction in the play is subordinated to the physical realism of the film. For example, the film omits the direct address to the audience that the town gossips, Beulah and Dolly, have in the play, and that serves to "set the nonrealistic key for the whole production" (p.15). Instead, the dialogue and action occur in the credible realism of a conventional screen narrative. Thus, too, the title was changed from the allegorical *Orpheus Descending* to the more naturalistic phrase that Williams recommended, *The Fugitive Kind*. One finds the phrase in his short story, "One Arm" (p.11); it suits so many of Williams's characters, glorious outcasts compelled to the rootless life of the road.

Despite the change of title, however, the Orphic underpinning remains clear in the film. Val is still an Orpheus figure, bringing music, love, and vitality to a deadened Eurydice (Lady). Jabe Torrance is a cold, malevolent Death (especially

as portrayed by Victor Jory) and the vigilantes who hose Val
into the fire are appropriate Maenads. But the Orphic myth is
not as prominent in the film as in the play. This is partly due
to the psychological particularity given the characters, and
also to the greater variety of settings used in the film. Where
in the play everything occurs in the Torrance general store, in
the film Lady takes Val out to visit the ashes of her father's
wine-garden and Val has his most intimate conversation with
Carol in (that typical Williams setting) the "bone-orchard"
(cemetery). Moreover, the film opens and closes with shots of
the open road. The literary myth of Orpheus is thus woven
into the film myth of the vagabond who has taken to the road
to cultivate and apply his power and integrity.

The second major alteration in the film involves the pro-
portion of scenes involving Val Xavier. As Lumet has remarked, the problem in the play is that Xavier is absent from most
of the last half, making it an *Orpheus Descending* without the
Orpheus.[1] In the film Lumet increases Val's visibility and his
influence upon the other characters. First, Val is played more
as a human being than as an ethereal phenomenon; this is
consistent with the realism of the adaptation. In the play Val
first appears as though summoned by the wild Choctaw cry of
a conjure man, after the women of the town have had the
stage to themselves to fill in the necessary narrative background. But in the film Lumet introduces Val first; only
through Val do we meet the town. The emotional effect is to
make his fate all the more horrifying, for it is a human figure,
not an abstraction, that is suffering.

Lumet also makes Val more of an influence upon the other characters. Where in the play Lady's confectionery is
present from the beginning, "shadowy and poetic as some in-
ner dimension of the play" (p.11), in the film it is introduced
later, as if Lady's determination to revive her father's dream
world were one result of her revivification by Val. Similarly,
in the play Vee explains the forces behind her painting to the
town gossips, but in the film her articulateness is drawn forth

by Val. Marlon Brando's Val, then, is more powerful in his action both upon the other characters and upon the audience.

Of course, the fact that the film is more realistic than the play does not mean that it eschews the poetic altogether. In the first place, the film retains the poetry of Williams's dialogue, particularly in Val's speech with his weird analogues and anecdotes.

A further poetic dimension is supplied by some exceptional photography. At one point Val tells Lady about a transparent bird that has no feet so it can never come to earth. The bird serves as the image of his own nature, restless, unable to land; he also yearns for the incorporeality of the transparent bird. As the scene begins, it is night, but there is a strong light outside the window behind Val. As he spins out his fable, the room darkens around him, until only Val's eyes are lit. When Val's story is over, the original brightness resumes. The lighting suggests that Val's vision is the sole illumination in the scene. Here Lumet and his photographer, Boris Kaufman, avoid what has been called the tyranny of film realism; they incorporate a dramatic effect into the realistic tenor of the work, inflecting the realism to heighten the expression. Such discretion would have well served the film of *The Glass Menagerie*, as we have suggested. Similarly, Kaufman gave the cemetery scene a combination of constant smoke and intermittent light, from passing cars, to express the duality of the play, the Lethe-al aspect of Two River County, where the action is set simultaneously on realistic and allegorical levels.

The film also develops a pattern of imagery of the elements— water, fire, earth, and air—to suggest that the drama of Val Xavier's life is something larger than a human story. For instance, Val arrives in town at the height of a rainstorm. And whereas Jabe boasts of a destructive force of fire ("We burned him out"), Val puts his claim to be a powerful lover in terms of fire: "I can burn a woman down." The paradox here is that Val's "burning down" of Lady revives the passion and fertility that she lost when Jabe burned down her father's arbor. Carol Cutrere, on the other hand, is a creature of earth, soiled and dark, and with a physical simplicity to her present pleasures and ambitions. Carol responds to Val's physicality immediately. But Lady tries to ignore it—"You don't interest me any more than the air you stand in"—before eventually succumbing to him.

The climax to the imagery of the elements occurs when Val is destroyed by the combination of water and fire. The townspeople drive him into the fire with their waterhose. In the play, Val is killed (but first castrated) with a blowtorch. In the more discreet London production, he was torn to pieces by dogs (offstage). But the combination of hose and fire in the film provides for a death by opposite forces, as if Val were too powerful a figure to be destroyed by a single element. Fire and water must combine to drive this lover out of his snakeskin and into ash.

Further to confirm the mythic resonance of the story, there is the pattern of cyclical recurrence. For one thing, the action begins and ends with shots of the road, where Williams's fugitive kind exult in their freedom but where even the transparent birds are doomed to fall. When Carol describes the tawdry pleasures of "jookin'," Lumet follows her with a 360-degree pan of the camera as she paces around, hungrily seeking roads to wander even indoors. But in this film, as in myth typically, roads lead back to their point of origin: Carol's performance ends with a slap from her brother. In the same vein, Val refuses to drive Carol to New Orleans because he wants to escape his past: "That's where I come from, not where I'm going."

But Val's fate is ineluctable. Thus Carol will find ashes on his jacket *before* his final confrontation with Jabe and the townsfolk (ashes that Val picked up at the burned wine-garden). Every hope of resurrection in the film is shadowed by the recurrence of tragedy. So Lady will twice lose her love and her baby to Jabe's hatred and his fires. And wherever the artist-lover may roam, incipient in the vitality and liberty he brings to others is his own annihilation.

There are two characteristically Lumet themes in the film. For one thing, Lumet is attracted to works about characters who cannot transcend their egotism: *The Group, Long Day's Journey into Night, Twelve Angry Men, The Pawnbroker, Last of the Mobile Hot-shots, Serpico.* Secondly, the Lumet hero struggles to escape his past to create a new life. This theme informs the changes he made in adapting *The Group, Bye, Bye Braverman*,[2] and *Murder on the Orient Express.* It is given a precise imaging in *The Fugitive Kind.* In the pretitle sequence, Val is revealed in a jail cell; the first image of the film is the wire grid of the lock-up. Vee Talbott lets Val sleep in another lock-up that has the same grid pattern. But the trellis in Lady's confectionery also has that grid which suggests her obsession with reopening her father's tavern, with spiting Jabe's malice—an obsession that prevents her from fleeing to start a new, fertile life with Val elsewhere. Lady's romantic nostalgia is her own kind of prison.

Finally, one might note one way in which Lumet emphasizes the personal involvement of Williams in the drama. The play's Jabe briefly objects to Lady's having moved the shoe display to the back of the store (before Val's arrival). Lumet gives the shoes more prominence. For example, the town teen-agers will flirt with Val over the shoes. Later, one of Val's tenderest scenes with Lady is played against the shelves of shoeboxes. Still later, when Lady exults in her pregnancy, Val leads her from the shoeboxes into her arbor. The shoeboxes represent the prosaic deadliness of life under the shadow of Jabe. After the fire there is a deep-focus shot of the store rubble. The familiar shoeboxes are piled in disarray in the foreground, as a kind of monument to the dead Val and Lady, but confirming the survival of the shoeboxes when the heroes have been destroyed. The neat order of the shoebox world has been upset, but its power remains. Of course, one of the best-known facts about Tennessee Williams's life is his drab job in a shoe warehouse. It is the very job that Tom flees in *The Glass Menagerie.* In this very incidental image, then, the film draws upon Williams's private symbolism and association—more discreetly than Brooks did in *Cat on a Hot Tin Roof*.

In such small ways, as well as in the larger commitments of character and theme, *The Fugitive Kind* is a creative adaptation of *Orpheus Descending*, at least as successful as the original. The film achieves a greater emotional impact by playing the original horrors against a more realistic surface. And it loses none of the play's context and thrust.

8

Summer and Smoke

(1961)

Peter Glenville's main challenge in filming *Summer and Smoke* was to accommodate the extreme stylization of the play to the realist requirements of the screen. A fine, powerful play, *Summer and Smoke* has two elements that work against easy filming: thesis characters and an expressionistic setting.

The play is perhaps Williams's most schematic work. It deals with the relationship between two neighbors who are not so much characters as embodiments of contrary principles. Thus John Buchanan, the doctor's son, is a pleasure-seeking sensualist. Even when he becomes a doctor himself, he personifies the physical nature of man. In contrast, Alma Winemiller is the minister's prissy daughter, whose very name means "soul." Williams establishes the debate between the two types in an opening scene, when the characters are children. When they have grown older, John attempts to introduce Alma to the pleasures of man's physical nature, which she rejects in favor of spirituality.

There is a turning point in John's life when, drunk and in debt, he agrees to marry the taverner's daughter, Rosa Gonzales. Alma phones John's absent father to warn him and when the senior Buchanan returns, he is killed by Rosa's father. John harshly attacks Alma for meddling in his life, but he assumes his father's medical responsibilities and gradually reforms. As John comes to appreciate Alma's values, she

67

begins to realize the vacuity of a strictly spiritual life. When Alma goes to John to accept his old offer of an affair, she finds that she has come too late. John is engaged to marry the young and lovely Nellie, once Alma's music student. The play ends with Alma in the park, picking up a traveling salesman, presumably the first in a long line of lonely lovers with whom she will seek compensation for her lost love.

Williams's set is as schematic as his characters. There are two interiors: the doctor's office, with its anatomy chart to represent the physical nature of man, and Reverend Winemiller's drawing room, to represent the isolated civility of the soul. But both interiors are only partially marked off from the outside by fragments of walls. Even the interior scenes are to be played under "a pure and intense blue" sky (p.9), as if man's distinction between body and soul were but a small fragmentation beneath the higher unity. Dominating the stage is a park, where a fountain statue of Eternity broods over the course of the play. Altogether, the set is a remarkably expressive but theatrical conception. It would not work before a camera accustomed to revealing real trees and sky—and the impression of real ceilings.

Glenville's achievement is a film that conveys Williams's themes but does not lose the effect that a film audience expects—the sense of real life passing before its eyes. To achieve this, Glenville did three basic things. First, he made his major figures more complicated, better rounded characters. Second, he opened out the action to include park concerts, outdoor walks, a car washing scene, casinos, and cockfights. Both these moves helped the film create the impression of life caught on the fly, instead of the thesis-drama that (quite effectively) occurred on the stage. Third, Glenville extended his physical settings into poetic metaphor, so that the evocative power of Williams's setting was modified but not lost.

First, though, the characters. Laurence Harvey as John Buchanan brings some weight to the character from his previous roles portraying men of strong ability and weak morali-

ty (*Room at the Top*). His vulpine elegance suggests a dangerous charm (*Butterfield 8, Darling*) that enables the viewer to
appreciate Alma's ambivalent interest in John. Producer Hal
Wallis originally wanted Montgomery Clift and Audrey Hepburn for the lead roles, but Clift would have lacked Harvey's
power and danger, while Hepburn's pert beauty would have
been inferior to the soft warmth of Geraldine Page (who
played the role of Alma in José Quintero's 1952 New York
stage production).

In addition to the shading Harvey brought to the role
from his continuing persona, the film's John Buchanan also
acquires some new business making him a more plausible
and intriguing character. Instead of coming to Alma's literary
circle, for instance, he is shown gambling at a cockfight. The
fighting birds foreshadow Buchanan's later remark: "I'm
hunting an elusive bird, Miss Alma. The bird of satisfaction."
At the fight he shows his blood-lust, a violent extension of his
sensual nature in the play. Moreover, when Buchanan later
takes Alma to a cockfight, one is puzzled by his motives, given
the psychological realism of the film. Why would the man
take the minister's daughter to a cockfight on their first date?
Why would he waste a Saturday night on her? Why would he
take her to the tavern where his mistress is performing?
There are two answers. Metaphorically: the man of physical
pleasure is introducing the spiritualist to his world in its most
extreme forms. And psychologically: the film Buchanan has
the streak of illogic, of inconsistency or inexplicability, that
characterizes human nature more often than literary types.

Glenville's outdoor scenes are also nice additions. The
street exteriors were shot on the old MGM sets that were built
for Judy Garland's *Meet Me in St. Louis,* so they have the
starched brightness of an idealized America, just the right abstraction for a debate between body and soul. It is also appropriate—both poetically and psychologically—for Buchanan to
lavish attention on his sports car, since his is the physical
transport of delight, and equally appropriate for Alma to be
summoned to cool him off with a hose.

Glenville also manages to animate the huge statue of Eternity that dwarfs the distinction between man's body and his soul. A static shape on the stage, the statue gains character and vitality in the film from the different perspectives taken by the camera. From the changes in our viewpoint, it gains different tones, different significances. For example, several key scenes are played at the foot of the statue, where its function is to serve as a lofty ideal. Thus Alma at first takes the cold stone to be the virtue to which man must aspire; she cites the analogous reach of a Gothic arch to the heavens. Alma is again in the shadow of the statue when she decides to be a woman for Buchanan, when she abandons her aspiration to be angelic. The only angel there is the statue: "Her body is stone and her blood is mineral water." At the end of the film, the statue seems to justify Alma's approach to the lonely salesman. Glenville draws back above the statue for his last shot, allowing us to share its beneficent gaze upon the casual lovers.

The film retains the symbolic values of the statue in the play. It brings water to the thirsty, as the concept of Eternity provides solace to the needy. Then, too, the stone of the statue represents the antithesis of the human flesh, as Alma—we have seen—comes to recognize. Man should not aspire to be statuary. If he does, the concept of Eternity can be deadening. Thus in the last shot of the film, the statue has not just water in its cupped hands, but the death image of dried, fallen leaves. As the water represents the solace Alma brings the salesman, the leaves express the death of her own romantic hopes. By coming closer and by moving around the statue, the film draws more varied and more subtle inferences than it could sustain in the play.

Of course, in the film the statue appears intermittently. It does not brood over the interior scenes. This is part of the destylization that the filming required. Glenville eschewed the blue sky over the interiors, but the sky and its remote blue remain Alma's emblems. She still tells John that she has looked through the telescope but not through a microscope, meaning that she has taken the long, ethereal view of man, not the close, physical one. In contrast, Rosa's father is given a colloquialism that expresses his lower ambitions: "The sky's the limit." Alma's wardrobe is dominated by blues of increasing darkness, to cohere with her association with the sky. In contrast, Rosa and Nellie, Alma's rivals for Buchanan, wear red. In this respect Glenville takes his cue from Williams's production notes, where he recommended "dramatic color contrasts" to the sky's blue (p.9).

While the film reduced the stylization of the play on the one hand, it extended its physical imagery into poetic effect on the other. The metaphor that the film develops most fully from the play is the smoke of the title. The precredit scene between the children opens on a smoke-filled Halloween. The fog filter and dry ice create an otherworldly atmosphere, as if the prototypal exchange between the characters were happening on a mythic level, for all time and all places. The smokey scene ends with the July Fourth fireworks, when we meet the characters as adults. Now the smoke has flares, if not yet any passionate fire. Later, when John has attacked Alma for meddling, the rectory to which she retreats is enveloped by smoke from burning leaves. The image recalls the characters' earlier scenes of affectionate meeting, but it also expresses Alma's gloom and confusion. As is cameraman Charles Lang's wont, the poetic effect derives from a natural, explicable source.

The smoke also retains certain significances from the play. For example, Alma tells John that her former self "suffocated in smoke from something on fire inside her." Her spirituality, in other words, was rooted in an unacknowledged physical passion. When John comes to believe in the soul, moreover, he describes it as "an immaterial something—as thin as smoke." He admits to his mistake in believing that Alma possessed "just a Puritanical ice that glittered like flame. But now I believe it was *flame*, mistaken for ice." Against the solid, cold stone of the statue, then, the smoke suggests the wispy, shifting transience of the human nature.

In addition, the smoke is the mystery of human warmth, by
which Alma will console the traveling salesmen. But it also
suggests the insubstantiality of man's angelic aspirations, and
the confusion to which cold saintliness may bring him. The
smoke by its association with fire expresses the passionate
nature of man. All in all, as an image of both substance and
insubstantiality, the smoke embodies the essential duality of
man, the physical and spiritual aspects that together form the
human being. That the same image, smoke, expresses both
the physical and the spiritual aspects of man proves their in-
divisibility and the fallacy of trying to live by one without the
other.

The smokey scenes in the film are offset by passages of
brilliant lighting. For example, at the cockfight the viewers
are sunk in darkness. When Buchanan leaps into the lit arena
to fight the recalcitrant bettor, it is as if he were leaping into
the light to find himself, as if he were plumbing the sordid experiences in search of self-definition, self-discovery. In this
way, the film often uses a single point of light to pick out a
character against a dark background, as if one's character can
be perceived only briefly against the mystery and smokey
darkness of man's composition. On the other hand, Alma is
given a mercilessly clear lighting when she is with Nellie and
Buchanan in his office at the end; Buchanan gallantly maneuvers Nellie away from seeing Alma's tears, but Alma has no
refuge from her exposure in the bright light.

In addition to lighting for mood, photographer Charles
Lang also lit the major characters in different ways.[1] Geraldine Page's Alma was shot with soft lighting, usually from a
three-quarter source that heightened the expression of her
eyes. The effect was to give her the beauty of radiance rather
than of striking feature. In contrast, bright, sharp lighting emphasized the sensual appeal of Rosa and Nellie. And sharp,
cross-lighting made Buchanan seem firmer, more jagged—an
angular, obtrusive figure. The film actor may lose the power
of physical presence that the stage actor enjoys, but his per-

formance can be inflected and deepened by such technical advantages.

In addition to these general changes in adapting the play to film, Glenville made a few other changes in his characters. For one thing, the Gonzales family was renamed Zacharias because studio executives feared offense to the Mexican community; however, Papa Zacharias was played by one of Hollywood's most familiar Mexicans, Thomas Gomez!

On a more important level, Glenville amplified the pattern of parent-child relationships from the play. All the characters have notable family structures. Rosa, for example, has a corrupt and corrupting father but no mother. Her parallel, Nellie, has no father but has a mother who runs a casino-cum-brothel, analogous to Rosa's father's tavern. Glenville stresses Nellie's sordid origins. These complementary family structures replay the motif of the human unit, where the body and the soul are interlocking opposites.

The same point can be observed in the major figures, with some modification. John Buchanan has no mother but an upright father, who has the ethical force to expel his wastrel son but also the sentiment to readmit him. Glenville gives old Buchanan (John McIntyre) a grim deathbed speech that shows him to be rooted in man's physical nature: "You are my seed, my posterity, all that I leave on this earth. Damn you!" The senior Buchanan is a gruff man whose good deeds are unleavened by spiritual idealization. He thus represents the virtuous limit of the materialist philosophy for which his son stands. But again, the casting of the familiar and appealing John McIntyre gives the character a warmth and humanity that save him from being a thesis-figure.

Alma is the only major character to have both parents. Her mother is embarrassingly self-indulgent; she steals luxuries (plumed hats) and is greedy for sensory delight (ice cream). In contrast, Alma's father is repressive. So Alma's parents replay the dichotomy of body and soul, instinct and conscience. But the characters go beyond this basic contrast.

For one thing, Reverend Winemiller is a spiritual man, but he falls far short of any ideal. He is insensitive toward Alma and his wife, and callously unforgiving toward John Buchanan. The film Reverend is crueler than the one in the play. For one thing, he refuses Buchanan's request to conduct his marriage to Rosa. The refusal is not due to Alma's concern for Buchanan, however, but due to his own hatred of the young man. Moreover, when the reformed Buchanan comes to call on Alma, the Reverend lies about her feelings and forbids Buchanan's return. The Reverend costs his daughter her last chance for respectable romance; in the film he even opposes her taking on the lowborn Nellie as a music student. In Reverend Winemiller, then, the film presents the wholly spiritual approach to life as a falsehood, a cruelty, and an arrogance.

Alma's mother represents the madness that can result from trying to live the Reverend's life. For she is quite mad —a babbling, incorrigible kleptomaniac. Nevertheless, Mrs. Winemiller expresses a great deal of wisdom. She appreciates Buchanan's romantic power and senses (and embarrassingly expresses) Alma's love for him. In her frustration at the jigsaw puzzle ("The pieces don't fit"), Mrs. Winemiller may be expressing Alma's frustration at trying to rejoin the disparate elements of the self, once they have been unnaturally separated.

Through this pattern of parents and children, man is defined as combining body and soul, the lowly origin and the lofty aspiration, with neither element able to fulfill a life by itself. Given the malice of Reverend Winemiller and the frustrated passion of Alma, there is no embodiment of pure soul in the film, because the soul cannot exist on earth without the body. Those who presume to be pure soul are either suppressing natural impulses (as Alma does and as her mother presumably did) or being cruel egotists (like the Reverend).

Thus when Alma goes to the salesman at the end of the film, she goes not in resignation but in joy. She takes a real interest in the lonely man. She will be a sister of mercy, not a fallen woman. For spirituality has its roots in man's physical nature. After all, her friend Roger Doremus's parents fell in love when they met in an infirmary, she with the mumps and he with dysentery! So Alma's quotation from the wicked Oscar Wilde—"All of us are in the gutter, but some of us are looking at the stars"—is upheld by the development of Nellie, the opposite resurrections of Alma and Buchanan, and the negative example of Reverend Winemiller.

In conclusion, it would seem that Glenville has sustained the poetic liveliness of the play, for all his reduction of its expressionistic effects. But there is one flaw in the film, which does not involve Glenville's adaptation so much as his incomplete familiarity with screen space—particularly with the expanse of Panavision—in this, only his third film. The characters are too often stuck in the center of the screen, engulfed by the wallpaper. At its best, this would express man's isolation; as Val Xavier remarks in *The Fugitive Kind*, we're all sentenced to a life of solitary confinement in our own skins. But in *Summer and Smoke* the image is repeated often enough and unvariedly enough to suggest not that it is a successful metaphor, but a failure in technique. Given the many and deep delights of the film, however, this single flaw is a minor one indeed.

A Streetcar Named Desire: As Blanche (Vivien Leigh) unpacks, her brother-in-law Stanley (Marlon Brando) begins to get ideas about her family fortune. © Warner Bros., 1951.

Cat on a Hot Tin Roof: A typically theatrical arrangement of the
Pollitt family. © *Loew's Inc., 1958.*

Summer and Smoke: Alma Winemiller *(Geraldine Page)* finds Dr. John Buchanan *(Laurence Harvey)* is engaged to Nellie *(Pamela Tiffen)*. © *Hal B. Wallis and Joseph H. Hazen, 1961.*

The Roman Spring of Mrs. Stone: Karen Stone (*Vivien Leigh, right*) begins her solitary descent through the stone streets of Rome. © *Warner Bros., 1961.*

Sweet Bird of Youth: The happy ending finds Heavenly (*Shirley Knight, in angelic soft focus*) restored to the battered Chance Wayne (*Paul Newman*). © Metro-Goldwyn-Mayer, 1962.

The Night of the Iguana: Reverend Shannon (*Richard Burton*) resists temptation (*Sue Lyon as Charlotte Goodall*). © Metro-Goldwyn-Mayer, 1964.

This Property Is Condemned: Owen Legate (Robert Redford) cools down some town sparks, as Willie Starr (Mary Badham) looks on. © Paramount Pictures, 1966.

BOOM: The dwarf security guard Rudy *(Michael Dunn)* towers over the imperious Flora Goforth *(Elizabeth Taylor).* © Universal Pictures, *1968.*

Last of the Mobile Hot-shots: Myrtle's wedding dinner *(Lynn Red-grave).* © *Warner Bros.-Seven Arts, Inc., 1970.*

9

The Roman Spring of Mrs. Stone

(1961)

José Quintero's problem in filming Tennessee Williams's first novel differed from those encountered in adapting the plays. For where a play has already expressed its themes through character, event, gesture, and setting—the kind of material that can be recorded on film—Williams's novel has a continuous narration, an explanatory voice that intervenes between the plot material and the reader. Nor is there as much dialogue in the novel as there is in a play, so the film maker must expand his characters' conversation, to keep their relationship lively, but without violating the characterization of his source. Quintero's first film generally succeeds.

Williams's novel traces the decline of a vain, faded, great lady of the American stage, Karen Stone (played in the film by Vivien Leigh). By playing roles for which she is too old (Juliet, Rosalind) and by having contented herself with easy, mechanical successes, she has compromised her art. Moreover, by marrying a wealthy old businessman for comfort and not for love, she has compromised her womanhood. Her husband dies when they are en route to a holiday. Mrs. Stone finds herself alone and drifting in Rome, which is characterized as a city of cold sensuality and prostitution. Though at first aloof from the tawdry world around her, she gradually accepts the attentions of a young gigolo, Paolo (Warren Beatty). He leaves her when a pretty, young starlet holds out the chance of a film career. Karen then abandons herself to a ragged young man who has been ominously following her throughout the action.

Karen Stone is antithetical to Blanche DuBois, Leigh's first Williams role. Both are women ultimately destroyed by callous men, but where Blanche was the violated creature of dreams, arts, and vulnerability, Karen Stone is the cold violator of art and of life. The "care" in "Karen" is ironic, for she has not cared for her art, her husband, her friends, or indeed for anything outside herself. But in the course of the story, her "Stone" turns to vulnerable flesh and blood. Like Alma Winemiller, Karen Stone opens herself to love too late. In her ultimate need for warmth and company, Karen, like Alma, abandons her prissy detachment to accept a sordid romance.

The other women in the story are foils to Karen. The Contessa (Lotte Lenya), for instance, is an aristocratic vulgarization of what Karen's art became, the sale of shallow romantic fictions. In addition, both the Contessa and Paolo, despite their poverty and prostitution, feel superior to the Americans; this provides a negative reflection upon Karen's presumption of greatness. Both ladies find their cultural heritage unavailing in their present humiliations. Thus, when the Contessa remarks that there can be no great ladies in a country only 200 years old, the film has her in a rather vulgar pose, with her feet up on her desk. Her vulgarity undercuts her pretense to dignity. Similarly, Karen's confidence in her scrapbooks of press clippings fails to keep Paolo when he decides to leave.

Karen is also contrasted to her friend, Meg Bishop (Carol Browne), a bustling, exploring journalist who still cares about her friends. By her energy, her will, and her interest in others, Meg avoids "the drift" that overwhelms Karen—"everything that you did without having a reason" (p.21)—and that Karen does not arrest until she accepts the ragged stranger as her lover.

Then there is the starlet (Jill St. John), who is still blessed by the beauty that has faded in Karen. Karen snubs the girl, which makes losing Paolo to her all the more painful. Despite her fatuousness, the starlet is more at home in Rome than Karen is. For the sweet bird of youth is a universal passport; the ancient city in particular hungers for youth and beauty. As Karen no longer feeds the hunger, she resigns herself to possessing it.

Our first sight of Karen is in the boy's costume worn by Rosalind in As You Like It. This may have been a touch of personal nostalgia for director Jose Quintero, for in his auto-biography he recalls that the first time he ever saw Vivien Leigh, she was in Viola's boy's costume for Twelfth Night.[1] But the image works within the film as well. First, by in-troducing the heroine in male costume, Quintero suggests an asexuality in her present nature. This is a faint equivalent to the section in the novel where Williams discusses Karen Stone's menopause and her relief from the dangers of child-bearing (pp.57-58). The film does not deal explicitly with Karen's menopause, except for Meg's veiled remark that "This time it's not a question of talent but—[pregnant pause] —time of life." The novel deals with the change in Karen's life more fully; indeed at one point it was to be titled Moon of Pause (the phrase remains, on p.50).

The second implication of Karen's costume is the sug-gestion of her masculine forcefulness. While Karen occasion-ally has an aggressive bearing, Paolo frequently seems ef-feminate, as when he preens himself and grows petulant at Karen's neglect. He, as she has done, will sell his beauty for a living. Paolo is also a projection of Karen's vanity. Thus, when she wants to be flattered about her new dress, he is absorbed with his appearance in his new suit. This hurts Karen, but it makes her aware of her self-preoccupation.

In contrast to the handsome, well-dressed Paolo, Karen's final lover is a grisly parody of the faithful fan. He follows her ardently, as if obsessed with serving her. In the film he does not insult her as crudely as he does in the novel, but his shabbiness and vulgarity are in contrast to Paolo's splendor.

In accepting this beggar, Karen abandons all pretense to being a great lady, in order to deal with her loneliness and isolation.

The implication is that the second man will murder Karen. As he picks up the key which she has tossed down to him, the sound track repeats Karen's earlier remark to Paolo: "A couple of years is all I need. After that a cut throat would be a convenience." When he drops the key in his pocket, there is a clink, as it hits something metallic, possibly the knife that Paolo predicted would prove her doom. The man's dirty smile is the last we see of him as his darkness fills the screen.

So the story is the tragic fall of a lady of fine art and beauty. Paolo and the Contessa both speak of Karen as "a great lady," with varying degrees of sarcasm, but Karen considers herself great. She sustains her high style even in the elegant way in which she wraps the key in a hanky to drop down to the ruffian. For, as is typical of Williams, there is a note of limited optimism at the end. Williams's heroes often find themselves when they are at the nadir of dissolution. They stoop to be most human; so there is triumph in Alma Winemiller's becoming a pickup, at the end of *Summer and Smoke*, for instance. And so Karen Stone comes to realize that "It was impossible, with dignity, to be anything but alone" (p.56), and she sacrifices her dignity. Finally, Karen Stone accepts a lover without pretense, without pride, but simply out of an honest need. This is the element of spring in Mrs. Stone's Roman descent.

For the most part, the film visualizes what the novel describes. Rome is depicted as predominantly stone, cold and unfeeling. The sensuality that Williams inferred from the physical setting—"Domes of ancient churches, swelling above the angular roofs like the breasts of recumbent giant women" (p.7)—is conveyed in the many shots of the people of Rome buying sexual favors: old men and women buying handsome or available young boys, the decayed courting the poor with a religious earnestness. There is virtually no vegetation to be seen in the film's Rome. Where it is not stone, it is glass, projecting images of company but without warm touch or security.

The film makes no mention of Karen's compulsion to dominate her male co-stars and her intensity at the childhood game of King of the Mountain. But these insights into her character are expressed in the shooting angles of her scenes with Paolo and the later lover. At first Karen is photographed standing at a higher level than Paolo, but as the power shifts, as he assumes control of the situation and she realizes that she had lost her former control, Paolo appears the higher. Similarly, from the moment that Karen throws down her key to the stranger, he looms over her.

Of course, the film cannot be exactly like the novel. Where it is, something is lost. For example, the film is unable to develop the pattern of bird imagery that runs through the novel, and by which Karen's characterization develops from fluttering spirit to predator. So when Karen buys Paolo his "dove-grey" suit in the film, the incident is true to the novel but the image has lost its meaning. As a kind of pointer to the pattern in the novel, however, we still get the Contessa's comparison of Karen to a chicken hawk, and the humans have the sensual rapacity conveyed by the bird analogue in the novel.

At its best, the film will elaborate upon an image from the novel, perhaps using it in a different place. For example, in the novel Karen is described as having clenched fists (p.70) as a metaphor for the stubbornness of her approach to a role. Quintero uses this image of Karen's rigidity elsewhere. When she first accepts Paolo as a lover, Paolo sits on her bed, takes her fist and unclenches it to kiss. The image works in two ways. Directly, Paolo is opening her up, relaxing her tense grip on herself, to make love to her. Secondly, there is a hidden pun in the gesture, for Paolo has offered himself to her in return for her monetary generosity, in return for her "open-handedness." The image works better, both as a pun and as an indication of her relaxing for Paolo, than the equivalent passage in the novel, where she opens her arms to him (p.59).

Similarly, Quintero expands upon the scene in the novel where Paolo invited the Contessa and the starlet to Karen's apartment to watch their home movies. In the film the scene develops a number of ironies. For example, the images of the past pleasure of Karen and Paolo are contrasted to their present tension. Thus the Contessa's "But where's Paolo?" relates innocently to his not having appeared yet on the screen, but also cattily to his having gone out on the balcony to arrange a tryst with the starlet. Moreover, the film images themselves suggest the futility of trying to preserve a moment of pleasure; the films outlive the pleasure that they record, but this makes for a painful viewing, not nostalgia. In addition, the home movies contrast the public image of the actress, Karen Stone, with her domestic life. In other words, the actress is not in those movies as an actress, but as a woman; the paradox is that these home movies still do not show real life, but a farce in which she has been romantically exploited.

The films have a sense of privacy about them, which the presence of Paolo's lady friends violates. For Karen Stone is conscious of being watched long after she has retired from the stage. Her new society teems with watchers and gossips. Paolo taunts her about the "spectacle" that she, like his earlier patrons, is making of herself. The public showing of her private movies is part of the shame Karen feels at having exposed her emotions.

Of course, the fact that we are watching a movie makes the home movie scene all the more dramatic. The image of a screen within a screen is a filmic way of depicting life within life, hidden sentiments or motives, layers of false appearance. At least twice the film audience is set up as intruding viewers, as violators of a character's privacy. The home movies is one example, of course, where we are with the Contessa and the starlet unwelcome witnesses to Karen's lost happiness. In the other case, we watch from a distance as the Contessa introduces another prospective gigolo to a client. The long shot frames the characters off in the cafe window. The frame and the silence recall the home movie screen. As we cannot hear what the characters are saying, of course, we peer all the more intently into their private scene.

Finally, the home movie continues as a physical assault on Karen's nerves. Her face is raked by the flickering lights from the screen, as an image of the discomfort that the resurrected memories cause her. And when the ragged lover comes to claim her, she awaits him on the dark left side of the screen, while in the right foreground the film projector runs on, the film ended but the machine continuing, flapping the film-end in a nerve-wracking, insolent way. Karen's time—like the false, flat, film image of her life—has run out. There is a similar moment in the novel, when, ushering the Contessa out after the home movie scene, Karen's "voice itself did not seem to belong to herself" but seemed to be part of a mechanical performance (p.125). Quintero's flapping film projector is a dramatic equivalent to that moment in the novel, where Karen's behavior is detached from her conscious self.

In addition to these minor inflections, two major changes were made to the novel. First, Quintero avoided the flashback form in order to dramatize the heroine's descent more directly. Where a novel can easily be contemplative and leap back and forth in time to select pertinent moments, film tends to suggest action in the present tense. A flashback in film works to suggest the present function of a past event. So the film begins with Karen's last stage performance, then her husband's death, then Karen's continuing descent to self-discovery.

The second change is the virtual omission of the narrator. This is traditional in the filming of a novel, where the visualization makes a running commentary unnecessary. But on this point, two further reflections need to be made.

First, without a narrator to guide our perspective, we tend to assume the perspective of the character whom we see the most, Karen Stone. The film focuses on her experience, with nothing outside it coming into view. Moreover, Karen's attitude is expressed in the shading of the material. For example, in the scene where Karen first meets Paolo, we do not see his face for some time. Instead we see him slouching deep in his chair, with his legs provocatively spread (the novel refers to his "odalisque poses" on p. 32). The scene thus expresses Paolo's sexual arrogance, but only from Karen's perspective. That is, it does not say "Paolo is arrogant," but rather, "Karen is struck by Paolo's arrogance." Further, that Karen does not note his face for so long suggests that her first interest in him is crudely sexual. Of course, she sneaks discreet glances at him throughout the scene without betraying her interest, but the subjective camera work exposes her.

Second, although for the bulk of the film the narrator has been omitted, there is a male narrator speaking over the opening scenes. An opening narration is something of a trademark of producer Louis de Rochemont. It serves to convey "information": that Karen has chosen a historic setting for her "posthumous existence," that she is living a drifting, widow's life; that her nemesis, the beggar watches her "as if waiting to give or to receive some secret signal"; and that "self-knowledge was something Mrs. Stone had always managed to avoid."

But the narrator serves more dramatic purposes. First, he reminds us of the interior analysis that the novel provided and that the film will leave us to do for ourselves. Second, what the narrator says is less important than the tone in which he says it. He speaks with the measured elegance of an Englishman. However knowing, then, our guide is himself an outsider, and the Rome we will see is the vision of an outsider. Third, there is sometimes a discrepancy between what the elegant narrator says and what we see. His detached elegance seems remote from the stone stairways and the shots of sexual soliciting. So, too, on his mellow phrase, "or to dream," we see a homeless youth asleep, sprawled across the city steps as if he were making love to the stone. Thus the narrator demonstrates the disparity between man's placid intellect and the squalid needs and ignoble satisfactions by which man survives. This, of course, is one of the implications in the great lady's resignation to the ruffian.

And finally, the presence of a narrator acknowledges the film's origin in Tennessee Williams's novel. The liberties that Quintero takes with his material are all minor, all creative, and all faithful to Williams's text.

10

Sweet Bird of Youth

(1962)

Richard Brooks's film of *Sweet Bird of Youth* returns us with a jolt to the Hollywood compromises. The producers were attracted to the sensational values of the play, but lacked the courage to present them as found. So the play was completely subverted. Williams's themes are the evanescence of youth and beauty, vigor and hope, purity and idealism; the corruption of the world; and the viciousness of man, whether from power or from impotence. But either Brooks or the producers preferred to make the familiar—and therefore safe—point that love is to be preferred over ambition.

The play centers upon three faded beauties. Chance Wayne and Heavenly Finley were ideal young lovers, but father Boss Finley sent Chance off to make his fortune in New York, contending that he was not good enough for Heavenly. Now Chance is an aging, corrupted gigolo. And on his last visit home, he infected Heavenly with a venereal disease. She plans to wed the doctor who sterilized her. Chance's last hopes for success are vested in Alexandra Del Lago, a faded old movie star, who buys Chance's favors with the illusion that she will star Heavenly and him in a new film, *Youth*. At the end of the play, Alexandra has abandoned Chance, Heavenly's sterilization has been made public, Boss Finley has been exposed as corrupt and sexually impotent, and Chance is about to be castrated by Heavenly's brother. Youth, sex, and vitality are destroyed both by the natural process of age and by the unnatural viciousness of man.

As he usually did when dealing with such sensational material, Williams (and the play's director, Elia Kazan) used a great deal of stylization in *Sweet Bird of Youth*. Alexandra Del Lago often addresses the audience directly, for example, even to challenge what she has said to a character ("Did I say that? Did I mean that?"). Further, a giant screen was used for Boss Finley's televised political rally. And in Act II, Boss Finley stages an elegant eighteenth-century masque with Heavenly, as a courtly reminder of a time forgotten, or a relationship that might have been. As other film makers did before him, Brooks omitted these theatrical stylizations in favor of a naturalistic narrative. But he did not provide anything to replace it, the way Peter Glenville, for example, provided deeper characterization for *Summer and Smoke*.

From Kazan's Broadway cast, Brooks kept Paul Newman as Chance, Geraldine Page as Alexandra, Madeleine Sherwood as Finley's mistress Miss Lucy (another beauty on the wane), and Rip Torn as Tom, Finley's sadistic son. As Boss Finley, Sidney Blackmer was replaced by the riper Ed Begley, whose persona of political corruption extended from *Twelve Angry Men* to *Advise and Consent*. But by now Paul Newman was the dominant star (his salary rose from $17,000 for *Cat on a Hot Tin Roof* to $350,000 here). Unfortunately, Brooks does not play against Newman's star image; instead he simplifies the play to enhance the character.

For example, in the film Chance Wayne has a more open and conventional response to the news of his mother's death than in the play, where he simply turns away from the speaker. And again: in the play it is Chance who falls in a drugged stupor in the hotel, while in the film it is Alexandra. And when Chance meets his old pals in the hotel bar, the film omits their ridicule of him; Newman's Chance is played closer to the hero's star image than the play requires.

Wayne's simplification is clearest in the matter of Heavenly's disease. In the play Heavenly has been sterilized, hollowed out, to cure her of Chance's gonorrhea. But in the film she has merely aborted his child. For a 1962 American movie, this may have been brave, but an important metaphor is lost in the translation. For Williams's Chance Wayne contaminated Heavenly with his own prostitution. His "profession" of love has poisoned even his idyllic love-making, so that now he can only implant poison and sterility. But in the film Chance can still plant life; sadly, the industry was not mature enough to present a star like Newman in a role so harshly drawn.

The film seems undermined by the very philistinism anatomized in the play. Thus the castration at the end is ... castrated! Chance's castration climaxes a series of references to Finley's failing potency, Finley's violent reaction to this loss, and his people's paranoid castration of an innocent black man. The castration, then, represents the envy and hatred that the ugly have for the beautiful, the poor for the rich, the old for the young, the impotent for the able. The film, however, omits the references to the black victim and ends with a mild phallic threat. Chance is spread-eagled over an automobile hood under Tom Finley's menacing cane. But when the "lover boy's meal ticket" is smashed, it is his face. Lest the shattered nose be taken as a conventional shorthand for castration, the film makes the ending completely happy. Chance and Heavenly go off together (a consummation for which a broken nose may devoutly be desired), and everyone turns against Boss Finley: Heavenly's Aunt Nonny, the governor, and the people!

This optimism pervades the film. Thus Miss Lucy gets a fresh start in life as Alexandra's driver, whereas in the play the actress had a police escort out, and Miss Lucy was abandoned. And even more strikingly, Brooks changes Alexandra's success in her Hollywood comeback. Williams described it as "a little, very temporary, return to, recapture of, the spurious glory" (p.122). But in the film she has a new career based upon her true self, her collected wisdom and experience. Her youthful beauty has been replaced by something better, she learns, while a college band plays smartly outside her window! In the film the sweet bird of youth and innocence has not flown away; it has been caught and caged. Age, debility, and corruption have been conquered.

Clearly this is not Williams's play, but an impostor. For over the course of Williams's eight versions, the play grew bleaker. Williams even changed the name of the actress from "Ariadne" to "Alexandra," thereby removing any hope that the hero would be left a thread to guide him out of his labyrinth. And the film mangles the one hopeful resurrection that does occur in the play. Williams's Alexandra begs Chance to leave with her, for he has revived the capacity for selfless sentiment in her frozen heart. But in the film this scene occurs after Tom Finley has threatened Alexandra if she does not get Chance out of town; in the play her invitation to Chance preceded Tom's visit. In the film, then, her emotion is adulterated by fear and self-concern, and Williams's point is lost.

Some of the play is nicely served by the film. For example, Brooks broadens Williams's social observation in the gallantries spoken by his villains ("You drive carefully now"; "You come back and see us again real soon"). He adds two scenes of back room politicking. In one, Finley pressures the chairman of the Daughters of Dixie, the mayor, the police chief, and the newspaper editor. In the other, Finley's liberal opponent reluctantly agrees to some unattractive skullduggery. Brooks supplies a fuller social canvas behind the action, perhaps correcting what even Williams took to be a fault in the play, a strained social background. [1]

Brooks also handles Williams's theme of false attraction rather well. On Alexandra's dressing gown, for example, flames burn at the hem and reappear to clutch at her bosom. But she offers only the image of passion. In her love-making, she is as cold and calculating as Boss Finley is in his politics and as Chance is in his prostitution. As Chance describes his career, the women in his past appear as cameo inserts over Alexandra, as if she were another in the series of interchangeable women to be exploited. The irony, of course, is that Chance is the replaceable figure in the ladies' lives. In the tangle of lust and manipulation, it is impossible to discern the true feeling from the false, or the hunter from the prey.

In one of the flashbacks, Chance tells Heavenly about the merry-go-round that will take him to the top. Behind him stands the spiral staircase that he descended to get to Heavenly. Here word and image combine for a fine irony. The real spiral that brought Wayne to his love contrasts with his illogical fantasy of a merry-go-round that will take him to the top—merry-go-rounds, of course, go around, not up. Hollywood ("like no place on this earth") is not his celestial path toward Heavenly, but an infernal distraction from her. Then Brooks holds on Heavenly's hurt face as Chance remarks that his past year was profitable for him, given the tricks he learned. She hugs him, but he has his back to her. Clinging to his spiral banister, he says "Don't ask me to give up my dream." This entire scene is subtly conceived but essentially wrong-headed. For Brooks's Chance turns his back on Heavenly to pursue his ambition, whereas Williams's Wayne has no ambition but to win Heavenly. He would not tell her not to come between him and his dream, for she is his dream.

In this scene, as in the others, Brooks converts an original vision of human decay and degeneration into a platitude about ambition. A tragedy of poison has become a romance of rebirth. In defense, Brooks claims that the producers insisted that the hero get the girl at the end. Brooks himself devised a different ending, which would have retained the bleakness of the play without its stylized monologue. Lucy and Alexandra were to escape, pausing on the ferry to light cigarettes. The ferry was to pause, to let a garbage scow pass. There, sprawled across the garbage, would have been the battered Chance. The studio rejected this ending.[2] But in having Miss Lucy leave with Alexandra, Brooks was already brightening and simplifying the original. And his addition of the staircase-merry-go-round discussion has nothing to do with the ending imposed by the producers. So how faithful Brooks's free adaptation might have been remains open to question. It would appear that the project was doomed from the outset.

And yet ... and yet, Williams himself has remarked that the film "was probably better than the play."[3] Clearly, even after all his revisions, Williams must not be satisfied with his play.

11

Period of Adjustment
(1962)

The collaboration between Tennessee Williams and Elia Kazan might have made an important play out of *Period of Adjustment*. Kazan was to have directed the 1960 New York production of the play, but he withdrew. Williams chose director George Roy Hill, on the strength of his musical, *Greenwillow*. The choice proved unfortunate, because Hill failed to develop the shadows and depths that lay beneath Williams's comedy; at least in Hill's film version, the play was trivialized.

There are traces of a new political concern in Williams's play. Two couples discuss their crumbling relationships and their unsteady selves, while their house and neighborhood sink into the ground. Indeed, the characters grapple with their personal anxieties heedless of the fact that their entire community is literally sinking into the earth. Kazan might have drawn this political concern more clearly than Hill did.

The film presents the two broken marriages from the play. In one, Dorothea Bates (Lois Nettleton) leaves her husband Ralph (Tony Franciosa) after six years of marriage, when he quits his job at her father's dairy company. In the other, a variety of tensions have spoiled the honeymoon of George and Isabel Haverstick (Jim Hutton and Jane Fonda) —fatigue, his having quit his job without telling her, and various smaller disagreements. On Christmas Eve, the Haversticks drop in on Ralph Bates, who was George's old Air

Force chum. Ralph counsels them; in return, they support him against his in-laws, the McGillicuddies (John McGiver and Mabel Albertson). Both couples are reconciled at the end.

This light comedy is not as great a departure for Williams as one might think. For one thing, he always laces his intensely dramatic situations with humor. Secondly, he may start with a comic genre and situation here, but he stiffens the play with some of his somber themes. For example, when Ralph tells Dorothea that "the human heart would never pass the drunk test," he could well be paraphrasing the film Blanche DuBois: "A line can be straight or a street. But the heart of a human being?" And Isabel's reflection upon marriage—

> What an awful frightening thing it is! ... Two people living together, two, two—different worlds!—attempting—existence—together!

—recalls Val Xavier's image of man locked in solitary confinement in his skin. Williams himself admits that the play is hardly "a happy play," but "about as black as Orpheus Descending, except that there was more tenderness, perhaps, less physical violence."[1] In any case, we should expect a Williams comedy to express the same vision as his darker plays, because, as he remarked in his "Prelude to a Comedy,"[2] an artist cannot simply turn off his vision; art is the inevitable, compulsive expression of one's life experience.

The basic vision of Period of Adjustment is given in the play's subtitle, High Point Over a Cavern. The basic theme is the hollow foundation on which man and society have erected their edifices of shelter and security. For the Bates home is in a subdivision that was built over a cavern, so the entire neighborhood is sinking. This metaphor opens out a number of important themes.

First, the community conspires to escape by keeping secret the facts of the sinking while the members sell out, in alphabetical order, to reduce their losses. This fraudulent silence is, Ralph admits, "disgusting but necessary." The point is picked up in the incidental conversation on the western on the television:

> You want an *honest* answer or a *comforting* answer?
>
> Give me the honest answer.   *(p.85)*

But the community prefers the lie. This social theme is given a personal parallel when Ralph approves the "temporary obfuscation" that liquor provides.

Second, the hollow base suggests the theme of false security. For example, marriage is a hope for security that is based on an absence of knowledge, a kind of void:

> *Isabel:* I'm afraid I married a stranger.
>
> *Ralph:* Everybody does that.

In addition, both Ralph and George lack confidence in their manhood so they strive for the appearance of power.

Third, all mention of career in the play is based on hollow hopes. Isabel was a nurse who fainted at the sight of blood; her profession was clearly unsuited to her nature. Both George and Ralph come from different places named High Point, but for both of them, their present High Points and their present jobs are disappointments in light of their past high points, when they were heroes in the Air Force. Now George plans to raise longhorns in Texas, but even this return to the earth has an airy twist: the cattle are for TV westerns. In something of a summary, the more level-headed Ralph admits that his house is built on a *"Cavern: yes!—a big subterranean cavern, but so is your project, not to mention your marriage!"* (p.77).

Fourth, the quivering earth has a psychological correlative in the characters' various nervous problems. For example, George was hospitalized for nervous tremors that have "no physical basis." Dorothea also shook, as Ralph recalls:

> Why, the night I met her, I heard a noise like castanets at a distance.... Then I noticed her teeth ... were chattering

together and her whole body was uncontrollably shak-
ing!   (p.27)

The virgin bride, Isabel, is so preoccupied with her own anxieties that she fails to hear Ralph's repeated explanation of
the geological problem (pp. 22, 54). Psychologically, as well as
professionally and physically, our security is based on a hollow base. We all have our caverns, one of the worst of which
is our insensitivity to those of others.

These implications of the cavern motif in the play are
worth examining at such length because the theme is virtually
omitted from the film. Passing references are made to the un-
stable housing, but the metaphor is not developed, not related
to the characters, and not visualized. Director Hill polishes
the veneer of lightweight comedy as if he were impervious to
the play's somber undercurrents.

The entire production betrays an insensitive touch. For
instance, the film opens with light, comic music but nothing is
done to suggest irony or deeper import. Moreover, the precredit sequence, that shows George and Isabel meeting,
courting, and wedding, violates the play in two important
ways. First, its speeded-up mime might suggest that tremors
are just a comic convention of human movement, rather than
the problem for which George was hospitalized. Second,
whereas Williams opened with two marriages quaking, the
film opens with one marriage quaking and one marriage beginning to take shape. In the play we discover the void beneath the edifice, but in the film we watch an edifice being
built over a void; the result is radically different. Finally,
Hill's comic invention is both weak and inappropriate. The
wedding supper at the truckers' cafe and Isabel's drenched
arrival at their motel may establish George's insensitivity, but
such slapstick imperils our interest in the psychology of the
characters.

On the other hand, there are at least two good touches in
the film. First, Hill exploits the hearse that in the play we are
told George bought secondhand for his honeymoon. The

hearse is a comic example of George's impractical prac-
ticalities, but by showing it, Hill converts every image of the
trip into an allegory about the Road of Life. Moreover, the
Bateses have their final quarrel in the front seat. They assume that they cannot be heard by the Haversticks, who are
sitting in the back, reconciled. The image is that of couples in
their own compartments, but with privacies that are shared,
connected, and mutually revealing. Sadly, such sensitive use
of the material is rare in this film.

Hill's second successful business involves Williams's
theme of false, swaggering manhood. Hill makes the Bates
dog a male named Bessie, that sleeps with the light on, is
afraid of the dark and of other dogs, and cannot find its way
home. The dog is almost human. Then, too, Hill gives Ralph
some sensible lines about manliness:

> When are you and a million other guys in this country go-
> ing to get over the idea that the real he-man is a big loud-
> mouthed ape, huh? ... When are you going to stop playing
> Superman, boy?

This is a fair addition, but it poses two difficulties.

In the first place, Ralph is inconsistent. After all, he has
been worried about his son's sissification, that his son may
not grow up to possess the conventional image of manliness.
Moreover, immediately after giving George the advice about
manliness, he appeals to George's macho egotism: "Or you'll
end up George Haverstick the last. End of the line. Obsolete."
He seems to assume that manhood is proved by having a son.

Second, while the play would agree with Ralph's advice,
the film does not. In the play the quarrels are between weak
and frightened people, but Hill treats them as—to quote the
sign behind the Haversticks in the service station—a "Power
Test." The film seems to share George's sexual nervousness.
Thus Hill adds a scene where George, on his solitary walk,
passes a little girl and boy   "You're dull," says the girl, but
the boy follows her earnestly: "Please, Margie."   and the
chains from the playground swings shadow George's face.

Here Hill strains to validate George's fear of women and en-
trapment.

Similarly, Hill has Dorothea's mother constantly con-
tradict her husband until he rebels. McGillicuddy tells his
wife to shut up, attacks her family's airs, and claims to admire
Ralph for standing up to him. The worm has turned. And the
film expects us to approve of McGillicuddy's rough recovery.
He salvages his dignity by asserting himself in the tradition-
ally masculine way, by verbal violence against his wife. This
Jiggs-and-Maggie relationship between the McGillicuddies is
itself a distortion of the play, and the father's "manly" recovery is a violation of its ethic. But the film expects us to ap-
plaud McGillicuddy for becoming the kind of man that Ralph
was teaching George not to pretend to be.

None of these changes were necessary elements of an adaptation to another medium, unless we assume that the film
audience cannot be given a comedy that raises serious anxieties. The failure, it would seem, lies in the interpretation of
the play, not in its adaptation to film. As a result, the film is of
less interest as a Tennessee Williams work than as a revealing early work by the director who went on to make such
commercial and macho successes as *Butch Cassidy and the
Sundance Kid* and *The Sting*.

12

The Night of the Iguana

(1964)

As one may or may not infer from the movie advertisements ("One man ... three women ... one night!") *The Night of the Iguana* is about man's search for God, the reconciliation of man's physical and spiritual natures, and—in Tennessee Williams's summary—"how to live beyond despair and still live."[1] The iguana is an ugly but tender creature of God, left to struggle against its tether while it fattens for death. It can be freed, if some other tender creature will choose to play beneficent God. But in the film, the iguana has man's perversity as well as his desperate constraint; finally cut free, the iguana stands there for a long moment, as if unable to realize that it is free to escape.

The human focus in the play is upon Reverend Shannon, a suspended priest who is now a tourist guide. Shannon brings his busload of Bible College women to the inn of his old friends, Fred and Maxine Faulk, where he hopes to rest and recover his equilibrium in Fred's pacific company. But, "Fred's dead." So for spiritual guidance Shannon turns to Hannah Jelkes, a plucky spinster-artist who is traveling with her senile poet-grandfather, Nonny. Hannah declines Shannon's invitation that they travel together, but she gives him the courage to accept himself as he is. At the end, Nonny completes his last poem—in which he yearns for the courage to face the harshness of the heavens and the corruption of the soil without a cry, prayer, or despair—and dies. Freed from his compulsion to recover the ill-suited grace from which he fell, Shannon settles down with Maxine.

Shannon's failure as a priest is due to his inability to isolate the (as he calls it) "realistic" level of logical, disciplined existence from the "fantastic" disturbances of life. Thus he is twice seduced and compromised by nubile young girls. Thus, too, his letter of submission to the bishop is drenched by his sweat and made illegible. Shannon's physicality dooms his attempts to be priestly. Theologically, Shannon shocked his congregation by attacking their conception of a harsh, negative God, whom they use to flay man for his instincts and his nature.

Shannon's sermon in the film teaches tolerance and self-acceptance, principles which are realized in the two sexual experiences that Hannah Jelkes recalls having had. In both Hannah braved shame in order to allow strange men their pathetic needs. Free of puritanical righteousness, Hannah's social kindness achieves what Shannon's religious activity failed to achieve, an open acceptance of the range of human possibility: "Nothing human disgusts me, Mr. Shannon, unless it is unkind or violent." Hannah's sexual experiences typify the salvation that Williams's characters so often find in deviance, on the sly, in the alleys or in the bars, wherever they can strike up a human spark against the cold, dark night. But Shannon, whether in the pulpit or as a travel guide, lacks Hannah's balance, so he too suffers shame and commits unkindness.

Though Williams has said that he dislikes the film,[2] it is true to the play, if one allows for the director's option of personal emphasis in his interpretation. For John Huston has always expressed a more robust spirit than Williams has, a vision less blackly lined with defeat and destruction and one where the joys of life and of the quest make up for loss and defeat. As a result, the film of The Night of the Iguana has a slightly more positive spirit than the play, although the essential themes of the original are preserved.

For one thing, Huston's settings are brighter than the

play's. The camera escapes the stuffy confines of the decaying inn for the lake in which Shannon and young Charlotte
swim, for the rich verdure around the inn, and for the mountain roads where Shannon has his compulsive driving spree.
These settings express the film's cheerier philosophy; they
suggest the preference for the fantastic world of man's senses
over the rigor of Shannon's religious "realism."

Huston also subordinates the horrifying to the comic. He
omits Shannon's story about old people rummaging through
excrement for food, for example. Then, too, the Shannon-
Charlotte scenes are played for the comedy of Nymphet Denied, instead of for the pathos of Celibate Seduced, and so we
are spared Shannon's postcoital anguish and penance. Huston also omits the "cherubic" Nazi tenants who holiday at the
inn in the original play. They represented the violence which
Shannon has suffered from others and to which Hannah's
perseverance has inured her. Huston replaces their implicit
villainy with the amplified malevolence of the schoolmarm,
Miss Fellowes, whose viciousness is on a smaller scale than
the Nazis' but is also more immediate. Moreover, removing
the Nazis allows the film to be set in the present.

This contemporaneity is important because much of the
film's power derives from the personae of its cast. For example, Richard Burton was a resonant Shannon because he
was considered a huge, wasted talent. Fresh from his epic
love story in (and around) *Cleopatra,* Burton was considered
the most gifted actor on the English-speaking stage, one who
was squandering his genius on booze, beauties, and the commercial fripperies of the silver screen. So Huston could omit
the habitual lustfulness of Williams's Shannon, because Burton's persona already expressed a fleshly weakness of heroic
dimensions. Moreover, as Charlotte Goodall, the seductive
minor, Huston cast Sue Lyon, who was famous for her one
role, the seductress of *Lolita.* Thus, quite apart from their esti-
mable performances, there was something of a mythic confrontation in Charlotte's siege of Shannon.

Perhaps the most important casting was Ava Gardner as

Maxine, the lusty source of Shannon's ultimate salvation, peace, and purpose. For Ava Gardner was once voted the world's most beautiful woman. Her romances and marriages were legion and famous. And twenty years after her heyday as a romantic lead, Huston found her still a stunning beauty. He was later to cast Gardner not just as a beauty but as Beauty, the archetype of natural pleasure and fertility, when she played Sarah in The Bible (1966) and Lily Langtree in The Life and Times of Judge Roy Bean (1972). But already in The Night of the Iguana Gardner is the Physical Life with all its elemental delights and energy. Ava Gardner's Maxine earns Shannon's compliment—"Maxine, you're larger than life"—in a different way than Bette Davis's Maxine did when Davis created the role on the New York stage (December 28, 1961).

Gardner's casting as Maxine is an important element in Huston's optimistic shift of the play. For one thing, the film Maxine is a far more positive figure than the one in the play. Huston's Maxine does not try to force Shannon back into drinking, does not threaten to have him committed again, and does not persist in her rudeness toward Hannah Jelkes (Deborah Kerr), all of which distinguish her from the original character. In the film, indeed, Maxine offers Hannah her inn, under the assumption that Shannon would stay there with Hannah. Robert Gessner finds this offer dramaturgically false,[3] but it seems to me to be consistent with the Gardner characterization as a generous fertility figure. The offer is even correct phsychologically, as Maxine senses Hannah's appeal for Shannon and may herself fear being refused by him.

Moreover, where the play gives Hannah the last word—and it is tired and resigned—in the film Maxine has the last word, and it is spirited and hopeful. "I'll get you back up, baby," she assures the exhausted Shannon, "I'll always get you back up." Gardner's presence thus vitalizes the role, cheers the play, and embodies the virtues of the hearty life. Indeed, as the poet Nonny works in the play as a model of

mind and will triumphing over time and old age to work out
his last poem, Ava Gardner's beauty denies the transience of
Shannon's "fantastic" life. Such resonance in casting, I have
suggested, is one of the characteristics that distinguishes film
from theater.

The final advantage of Gardner's casting is her spirit of
self-parody. From her extravagance, a jocularity spreads
throughout the film, shading the extremities of Burton's performance and helping to accommodate the juicy flourishes of
Williams's eloquence. The element of self-parody derives
partly from the Gardner, Lyon, and Burton personae and
partly from Huston's own style of humor, particularly as we
find it in *Beat the Devil* (1954) and *The Man Who Would Be
King* (1976).

As another aspect of Maxine's self-parody, Huston expands the function of her beachboys, Pepe and Pedro. They
are not given the menial labor they do in the play; in the film,
the Bible teachers' baggage is the white man's (Driver
Hank's) burden. Unimpeded by duty or conscience, the boys
frolic through the film as restless energies, where in the play
they were torpid. In the film they personify innocent pleasure. It is they who catch and tie the iguana. In a fight, they
defeat Hank with a dance. (Indeed, the elemental life ele-
vates everything to a dance. Thus Maxine will call dysentery
"The Aztec Two-Step.") As Maxine's lovers, the boys represent her energy and her capacity for life. Their constant music is joyous and simple, but there is something ominous in its
persistence, as if their innocence were not something to be
enjoyed by those lumbered with conscience. In any case, the
boys and the music help to buoy the spirit in the film, where
the play works in more melancholy rhythms.

Huston's other additions are reasonable extensions of the
text. For example, his precredit sequence shows Shannon
driving his congregation out of the church with his unorthodox sermon. This is more dramatic than the description
he gives Hannah in the play. It also enables us to appreciate
the man's power before his fall.

Of course, his work as a tourist guide is a continuation of his work as a priest: "tours of God's world conducted by a minister of God." Similarly, when Huston's Shannon stops the bus to watch the natives washing, a "moment of beauty ... a fleeting glimpse into the lost world of innocence," we recall that he works for *Blake's* tours, this traveler through innocence and experience. In his travel, as in his religion, Shannon trusts to his personal experience more than to the printed word; thus he tells Miss Fellowes that he knows Mexico better than the company brochures do. Then, too, the film shows that his present charges are like his former parishioners. They crave comfort and a harsh, efficient authority (like Miss Fellowes) instead of the unpredictable pleasures that Shannon might provide. Moreover, when they sing "Happy Days Are Here Again," they reveal their insensitivity to the suffering among them, Shannon's and their own, and the shallow cheer that is their "faith."

In another addition, Charlotte typifies the materialism and insensitivity of Shannon's congregation. "Are you really a man of the cloth, Larry?" she asks him in the film when he is swimming, and thus most obviously a man of the flesh. Then, too, her trinitarianism is her father's three Ford dealerships in Thunderbird Heights, which give Charlotte authority even over Miss Fellowes. Finally, one might remark upon Charlotte's blouse, emblazoned not only with the sweet bird of youth but with vipers as well. For similar though their life styles may be, Charlotte lacks the ethical base and the constancy that make Maxine the proper mate for Shannon.

The film's Maxine gains a further moral weight from her association with the departed Fred. Shannon regarded Fred as his "hope of salvation; all my chips were on him." Fred is a savior figure in the play, for he was spiritual, detached from the mundane world, and the one to whom Shannon looked for salvation. He had even lost sexual interest in Maxine, preferring to catch fish all day and throw them back into the water. Fred, then, reached a priestly peace by enjoying life. In the film, Shannon literally inherits the shoes of the fisherman and follows in his footsteps. He settles into the sensual comforts with Maxine from which Fred moved into his spirituality. As in the play, the religious movement in the film is away from the punishing divinity of the church and Bible College and toward life, art, and the fellowship of the flesh.

Huston confirms the theological implications in even the slightest details in the drama. For example, in the play Miss Fellowes phones Blowing Rock, Texas, to complain about Shannon, but in the film she calls Corpus Christi. As a result, the film, like the play, preaches the religion of appreciating life. Fred, Hannah, and Maxine are a secular trinity in a religion that operates not in the detachment of the pulpit, but in the squalid circumstances of human exchange.

For in the film, as in the play, the worst misery in the human condition is loneliness. In the play, Hannah and Shannon discuss the loneliness of traveling, even in a crowd. Hannah's response is to believe in even the momentary connection between people, "one-night communications ... outside their separate cubicles." Thus she defines a home not as a place but as a mental state, "something that two people have between them." Huston dramatizes this theme in the one scene where he allows Miss Fellowes a moment of our sympathy. He has her awake in bed, lying in her own netted cubicle. She apologizes to Charlotte, whom she supposes to be in the cubicle next to her. "You can afford to be generous," she says, ever conscious of her ward's wealth, "I was beside myself." The joke is that she is beside no one now; Charlotte is gone. But the scene is touching nonetheless, for it shows the villain in a rare moment of humility and it dramatizes the isolation of man.

The film seems to occupy a central position in Huston's film canon.[4] This is not because he changed Williams's play radically, but because the play basically suited his spirit. For example, in *The Treasure of Sierra Madre* (1947), the characters' quest for salvation is approximately the same as Shannon's: Curt adopts the murdered stranger's wife and Howard goes to care for the natives. Similarly, Huston's emphasis on the joy of living and the laughter at defeat, his comic response to a cosmic disappointment—as seen at the end of *The Maltese Falcon, Sierra Madre, Beat the Devil, The Asphalt Jungle,* and *The Man Who Would Be King*—is just an extension of the comic tinge found in even William's bleakest vision. Huston may laugh more robustly than Williams does in his work, but there is the same spirit in both men.

13

This Property Is Condemned

(1966)

Sidney Pollack's film is such an extensive expansion of Tennessee Williams's one-act play, *This Property Is Condemned*, that the credits justly declare the film to have been only "suggested by" the original. Yet the film is a remarkable evocation of Williams's imaginative world. Effective as an adaptation of the particular play, the film may perhaps best be regarded as a critical response to the entire Williams canon.

In the play, thirteen-year-old Willie Starr, wearing a grownup's gown and tawdry baubles, walks along the imagined tightrope of a railway track. She meets a boy out flying his kite. Willie tells him that she lives alone in the family's abandoned rooming house, where her older sister Alva used to be "the main attraction." She recalls Alva's fast life and her death from consumption, abandoned by all the men who had courted her. Now Willie has inherited Alva's dress, her baubles and boyfriends, and her delusions of a glamorous, romantic life.

The film opens and closes on this scene, with Willie (Mary Badham) on the railway tracks. But the body of the film is the story of Alva (Natalie Wood). Alva is exploited by her mother Hazel (Kate Reid), to attract men to the Starr boarding house. Alva's suitors include her mother's boyfriend J.J. (Charles Bronson), the shy Sidney (Robert Blake), and Mr. Johnson (John Harding), an elderly engineer with a sick wife.

Then the romantic stranger rides into town. Owen Legate

(Robert Redford) is sent by the company to close down the railway station and lay off the men. Legate soon confronts Alva with the sordidness of her flirtations and with the falseness of her romantic pretensions; however, she determinedly continues to associate with him even when her friends first ostracize, then physically assault him. Originally, Legate plans to take Alva away with him, but when he overhears Hazel say that Mr. Johnson will underwrite their new rooming house in Memphis in return for Alva's favors, he quarrels with Alva and leaves alone. Bereft, Alva goes with Hazel; however, in a fit of drunken candor, she exposes Hazel's and Johnson's pretenses to innocence. After spitefully marrying her mother's J.J., she deserts him the next morning. Eventually, Alva and Legate meet again in New Orleans, where they live in bliss until Hazel reappears and informs him of Alva's marriage. After witnessing Owen's shocked response. Alva rushes off in the rain. Willie reports that Alva died alone.

The film, then, fleshes out a story that is only hinted at in the original play. In addition, Pollack—with the help of the sixteen writers who reportedly had a hand in the project —takes two major liberties. First, he gives Alva one great passion, whereas in the play she passes from promiscuity to death. On one level, this great love is a box-office concession, but at another, it provides the film with its moral norm, for Legate is the moral as well as the romantic center of the film. Further, as we shall see, Legate provides a counterweight to Alva's romanticism. He proves the possibility of reconciling the romantic and the realistic visions, at least for a while.

The second change involves the composition of the Starr family circle. In the play the mother abandoned the home first, leaving the father to raise Alva and Willie. Then the father abandons the girls. In the film, however, it is the father, described as the kind of romantic vagabond that the Wingfield father was in *The Glass Menagerie*, who first departs. This railway man, like that telephone worker, fell in love with long distance. It is our first indication that Pollack's expansion of the one-acter relates to Williams's general canon.

Moreover, as critic Raymond Durgnat has pointed out, the family of the three females recalls the three faces of Blanche DuBois: the child-girl, the glamorous tease, and the aging hypocrite.[1] One can go further. For example, just as Kowalski forces Blanche to face the truth of her degeneration, so Legate teaches Alva to abandon her lying fancy. To point the parallel, the scene in which Legate draws Alva out of her imaginary world is set in The Honeydew Express, an abandoned railway car that her father had painted ornately and named "Miss Alva." It is to this car that Alva used to retire for her fanciful flights from reality, retreating (as it were) into a romantic projection of herself. And it is in this setting that Legate urges her to avoid glossing over reality. His traveling job, for example, is monotonous and he has no dreams. But his prosaic honesty marks the beginning of their love affair. So there is a parallel between the streetcar named Desire that Blanche rides to the end of the line to meet Kowalski, and the sidetracked, tawdry, and immobile railway car in which Legate begins his liberation of Alva—and Alva her warming of the dreamless Owen Legate.

As planned, the film would have echoed other works. For example, Pollack originally intended the film to end with Alva returning wet, bedraggled, and babbling about the white sky she had imagined in the Honeydew Express. She was then to pick up a traveling salesman (presumably Archie Kramer from *Summer and Smoke*). But the producers feared the film would have too many endings that way.[2]

Even so, there are many clear quotations from other works in the film as released. One is a parallel to the graveyard scene in *The Fugitive Kind*, where Val Xavier begins to restore Carol Cutrere's shattered self-respect. Legate's first assault on Alva's pretensions is set in a "ghost garden"; here he translates the "common politeness" that Hazel wants Alva to show the men, as "good business." Appealing to her sense

of self-respect he says: "If you really thought you were beautiful you wouldn't be anybody's property."

The film also develops another motif common in Williams's work: the difficulty that the sensitive character has
breathing, the struggle to draw freely upon the source of deep
life. Blanche DuBois, for instance, recalls the rattling breath
of her dying family. And she wants to marry Mitch because "I
want to *rest!* I want to breathe quietly again!" In *This Kingdom of Earth*, Myrtle has asthma and Lot has tuberculosis.
Similarly, in *The Night of the Iguana* Hannah Jelkes takes
deep breaths for the same reason that other people take
pills—to summon up the extra strength to persevere through
the afflictions in life. Williams's last stage direction in that
play has Hannah draw a "soft intake of breath" as she checks
whether Nonny is still breathing.

Pollack develops the breath metaphor in *This Property Is
Condemned.* Alva feels stifled by her small-town life. More
specifically, she frequently catches her breath, as at the sudden sight of the scarecrow in the garden. "The worst part
about being buried under the ground," she later remarks, "is
not being able to breathe." And in her early anger at Legate
she shouts "I hope you suffocate!" Breathing is among the
basic metaphors in Alva's characterization. She even dies of
what Willie calls a "lung affection," as if her emotional sus-
ceptibility were fatal; coarser natures survive, unfeeling and
unaware of the need for deep breath. And by developing the
metaphor of breathing, the film defines an important metaphor in Williams's other works.

A further echo of *The Fugitive Kind* can be found in the
pathetic way that Willie continues the forms of Alva's spirited
existence. Willie plans also to die of lung affection. By wearing Alva's gown and beads and by exercising her own pathetic imagination, Willie continues the line of doomed romance
the way Carol does when she picks up Xavier's snakeskin.
One generation of doomed dreamer feeds the next. Both Starr
sisters are in the tradition of Williams heroines—dreamers
struggling to impose a glamorous fantasy on the sordid reality

that abuses them. The house, the girls, the tradition of beautiful dreamers, all are properties condemned by the vulgar survivors of this world. Theirs is the fate of the romantic imagination in a world ruled by coarse realism. Thus it is to gloss over the failure of the world to live up to her dreams that Alva invents glamorous good times: "I felt that I was there. And that's just as good as being there."

In contrast, Legate does not seem like the Williams hero. He has the romantic aura of the rover but lacks the style of Chance Wayne and Val Xavier. For Legate's roving is related to his job; he is responsible, realistic, stable. Legate is coldly prosaic at the outset:

> Engineer: Doin' the things that you do, how do you sleep?
>
> Legate: On my stomach.

Where the Williams heroes are usually a force that opens and frees the communities they visit, Legate's job requires that he bring closure and death to the town. But Legate does free Alva. He replaces her illusions of satisfaction with the real thing. And like other Williams heroes, he represents the truth. Legate is accustomed to falseness in others:

> Hazel: A buck is a buck.
>
> Legate: If you're lucky.

Like Big Daddy and Brick, Legate has learned to expect the counterfeit. Thus he sees through Alva's pretenses immediately. And because he is himself a force of such honesty, he immediately befriends the candid Willie.

So Legate is rather more settled and sober than the usual Williams hero. He has the form but not the spirit of the fugitive kind. He is neither the peripatetic poet (like Xavier) nor the brutish realist (like Kowalski) but something in between. For in this film we do not have the classic confrontation between the practical realist and the dreamer. Here the realist (Legate) does not destroy the dreamer (Alva) in an open conflict, as often happens in Williams's work (for example, *A Streetcar Named Desire* and *Kingdom of Earth*). Instead the film dramatizes the effect that this open conflict has on the audience. Pollack gives the dreamer the superior power because the dreamer, not the practical realist, usually commands the audience's sympathy. Intellectually, one can understand Kowalski's position, but emotionally, the play belongs to Blanche. So in Pollack's film, Legate the sober realist is significantly softened by Alva's romantic influence.

Alva's imagination playfully pretends to make Legate a poet, when early in their acquaintance she catches him rhyming "pair" and "flannel underwear." But from such unpromising beginnings, Alva does achieve a poetry in Legate. True, he dispels her fanciful delusions. But she brings a romantic fullness to his life. Thus their reunion in New Orleans seems to affirm her romantic vision, for they meet against an all white sky, such as Alva imagined in the scene in the Honeydew Express. Her first words to him now are what she complained of earlier: "You have that habit of starin'." In his reply—"I'm sorry"—Legate apologizes both for having left her and for having probed too far into her pretenses. Later, in bed, he adopts her on her own romantic terms: she will stay with him, he says, because she gives him "Thoughts I never had. And things. Such things." This conversation is heard voice-over, as if it were not a matter of one character speaking to another, but of an understanding pervading the room.

Their affair at its height represents precisely what Legate tried to dissuade Alva from doing: imposing a romantic fantasy upon a coarser reality. Thus their idyllic interlude is set against wet and gloomy weather, of which the lovers seem oblivious. Earlier, when Legate tried to follow Alva in New Orleans they passed a laundromat named "The Washing Well," which seemed to suggest that even the most prosaic elements in Alva's real world were straining to conform to her fantasy. (The song which is her theme is called "Wish Me a Rainbow.") When the lovers finally meet, they see each other's reflection in a fountain, as if it were a wishing well and the world were making their wishes come true.

But the world does not make lovers' wishes come true, not in Tennessee Williams's vision. Alva's romanticism may be freed from lies and delusion by Legate's realism, and Legate's prosaic nature may be elevated by the touch of Alva's love and fancy, but their love ultimately fails because of Legate's "realism." For Legate abandons Alva twice. The first time is when he wrongly accuses Alva of Hazel's falseness and leaves town without her. The second time is when he registers horror at the news that Alva was married to J.J. In both cases Alva suffers from Legate's loss of faith in her. In both cases, too, Legate succumbs to cynical illusions about her. For the "fact" that she married J.J. does not make her his property, so it should not have condemned her to Legate's chill. Alva's love for Legate is a deeper truth than her marriage to J.J., but Legate—his very name now betraying his cold legalism—fails to sustain the grip that Alva sustains, on the deeper, emotional reality.

The power of Alva's spirit is expressed most dramatically in a shot that is the technical highpoint of the film. It occurs as Alva leaves J.J. to try to find Legate, or at least to start a new life in New Orleans. She has no confidence that she will find Legate, or that he would accept her if she did. She has only the spirit of her wish. The shot expresses her spirit, as her theme ("Wish Me a Rainbow") is given its first full statement.

The shot was taken from a helicopter. Beautiful to behold, it is too striking—and was too difficult to set up—to be merely ornamental. Alva mounts the train. The tracks whiz by; she peers out the window, pensively. Then the camera draws up, back, away from her, as her "Wish" song continues. The train is then shown in that aerial shot as it crosses a thin bridge over a huge body of water. By itself, this image suggests the crossing of a state of consciousness, as if Alva were moving from one plane of character to another by making this break with her past. Then the camera rotates through 270 degrees, so that the train, which began by moving left to right on the screen, moves downward, then right to left, then finally upward. The shot visualizes a character's reversal of her life. Its extravagance suggests the effort of will by which Alva is changing the course of her existence; she is, in effect, turning her world around. This Pollack's camera does on her behalf.

The visual rhetoric in this shot functions in a variety of ways beyond the ordinary means of literature and drama. For example, it isolates Alva in a vast space, suggesting her fragility and helplessness. Moreover, it makes her seem not to be in control of her own movement but swept along; she disappears in the train. So this shot works in antithesis to our first impression of Alva, when she seemed to be a free spirit but was actually being manipulated by her mother and used by the men. In the aerial shot, Alva's will and independence may be hidden, but they are expressed in the exhilaration of the perspective.

Finally, this shot can be contrasted to the last shot in the film in which Willie walks away down the railway tracks; the camera moves away from her along the ground, then rises and soars until Willie is no longer visible in the smokey, sunken landscape. The earlier, aerial shot of Alva in the train was a shot of escape from the world. But the shot of Willie, quite literally a "tracking" shot, expresses a flight within the world, but one still rooted in the sordid, physical reality. For without a Legate to go to, and without the maturity of spirit to animate her formal emulation of Alva, Willie's flight cannot be the soaring and the tragic success that Alva's was.

This one sequence and its ramifications may suggest the intelligence of Pollack's film. Perhaps Williams is somewhat hasty to claim that this "vastly expanded and hardly related film" took only the title from his "very delicate one-act play."[3] In the narrative frame, there is something like a fine performance of the play. But the greater interest lies in the way the play is expanded in the context of Williams's other work. For this film works the way a critical study does, by defining the relationship of the play to the author's major concerns elsewhere. The additions that Pollack drew from other Williams works function like the quotations in an essay—to set the individual work in the context of the author's overall canon. Pollack's film is a rare achievement: a strong drama that also works as a critical analysis.

14

BOOM

(1968)

The most cinematic of the Tennessee Williams adaptations is Joseph Losey's *BOOM*. Williams originally published the material as a short story in *Mademoiselle*, "Man Bring This Up Road." He rewrote it as a short play, *The Milk Train Doesn't Stop Here Anymore*, but it was, he says, "really only successful, scriptwise, as the movie *BOOM*."[1] Williams predicts that someday it will be recognized as an important film.[2]

Like the play, the film centers around a wealthy widow, Flora Goforth (Elizabeth Taylor), who commands an island empire from her opulent white marble villa overlooking the Mediterranean. She is visited by a roving poet, Chris Flanders (Richard Burton), whose habit of visiting people on the eve of their death has won him the nickname, "The Angel of Death." Upon his arrival, Flanders is attacked by the savage watchdogs and the sadistic security chief Rudy (played by the dwarf Michael Dunn); insulted and starved by Mrs. Goforth; and propositioned and then insulted by another houseguest, the Witch of Capri (Noël Coward). His only sympathy comes from Blackie (Joanna Shimkus), Mrs. Goforth's beleaguered secretary. Finally, Mrs. Goforth's furies subside, as she succumbs to her leukemia. She summons Flanders to make love to her but she dies as he comforts her in his arms. Flanders removes her precious jewels and sets them aside. Her most spectacular diamond he drops into a glass of wine, which he then pours into the sea. For in this drama it is the wealthy woman who is the predator, stealing the lives and energy of others; the penniless poet is a generous lover—and a comforting angel of death.

The film keeps to the basic situation of the play—Williams wrote the screenplay and attended the shooting in Sardinia—but develops an amplitude that the simpler and shorter original drama lacked. It is distinguished by an extremely literate and evocative script, by effective "filmic" casting, by an orchestration of significant sound effects, and by a spectacular, suggestive setting.

Williams's screenplay traces a shift in power from the wealth of Mrs. Goforth to the warm humanity of Flanders, who gives her

> this possibly timely piece of advice. That tough as you are,
> you're not so tough that one day, perhaps soon, you're
> gonna need someone or something that will mean god to
> you, if it's only a human hand, or a human voice.

Here, as in *The Night of the Iguana* and *Summer and Smoke*, religion is defined in the warmth of the human touch. So, too, Mrs. Goforth will feel Flanders's warmth "like radiation" through his robe. Though she calls him a "burned-out poet," she is herself "burnt out, like a house on fire"—wasted but still ablaze with her appetite for life.

Mrs. Goforth is an extremely lively character. She is contrasted to the shriveled dwarf Rudy and to the Witch, who is an anemic parasite:

> Are you still living on blood transfusions, Bill? Not good.
> Turn you into a vampire.

He is, as Mrs. Goforth notes, "the heart of a world that has no heart." He feels no pain:

> My heart beats blood that is not my blood but the blood of
> anonymous blood donors.

In contrast, the lively Mrs. Goforth is described as fully blooded:

Flanders: Mrs. Bloody Goforth!

Goforth: He's been shouting my name as if he knew me.

In an elegant, bloodless society, Mrs. Goforth is luxuriously vulgar, energetic, and bleeding to death, as she spots the floors with her coughing.

But for all her blood and energy, Mrs. Goforth is heartless. She is cruel to her servants, for example. Moreover, she is even guilty of the murder of a young peasant, whom she may have invited into her room as a lover. Finally, Blackie is another victim of Mrs. Goforth's parasitic energy, as she has exhausted and intimidated the girl into total submission. As much as the Witch, Flora Goforth belongs in the "elegant cold bloodless world" to which Flanders brings his visitations of warmth and generosity. Her real name may be "Flora" but the allusion to the goddess of springtime is ironic. The dry sibilance of her nickname, "Cissy," is more apt, for she is associated with sterility. The vegetation that surrounds her is restricted to brown thistles and weeds and a pineapple-shaped lamp by her bed. Even when she declares herself to be a free spirit, she stands against skeletal brown shrubs, a glass of tomato juice in her hand as an image of her bleeding death and her need for support.

These passages suggest the film's verbal and visual richness. There is also a remarkably expressive casting for the film. For example, there is the surrealism of casting a dwarf as a bodyguard and security chief. Michael Dunn is frequently photographed from a low angle or in close-up so that he appears to be a towering presence. This suggests a world in disorder, with values and priorities inverted; the shots have a disorienting effect upon the viewer, so that the idea of disorder and confusion is given direct, visceral expression.

Then there is Noël Coward as the Witch of Capri, a polished but emotionally stunted gossip. First, Coward's fame preserves our affection for his character despite his malevolence. The Witch may be a repulsive character on the page, but our familiarity with Coward makes him more agreeable.

Second, Coward personifies the delicious decadence of the aesthete, as is imaged further in the *objets d'art* in the villa—lumber without human attachment. Third, it is unsettling to see the elderly Coward so many years after his brilliance. So the Witch, like Goforth and like the aging Flanders, is an image of style in decay. (Rudy, of course, is life stunted and Blackie, life suppressed.)

The key castings, though, are Mr. and Mrs. Burton/Taylor, as the young man and the old woman of the play. Williams considers Burton too old and Taylor too young for the parts (which were played in Tony Richardson's production by Tab Hunter and Tallulah Bankhead). However, the casting of Burton is not indefensible, for in the original short story, Flanders is 34, claims to be 30, but is "a good deal older than he appeared" (p.58). The difficulty lies in the casting of Taylor and Burton together, for the age gap between the characters disappears.

The effect is a different, but harmonious, statement than the characters made in the play. The gap across which Burton's Flanders reaches out to Taylor's Mrs. Goforth is not one of age and experience, but one almost completely of class, power, and humanity. As a result, the film relates to such Losey works as *The Servant, Accident,* and *The Go-Between,* where Losey explored the human tensions across class strata. So while the casting of Burton and Taylor was probably due to box-office concerns, the aesthetic effect was to produce a more political statement.

Losey emphasizes the political element in the film by the attention he pays to the incident involving the murdered peasant. Mrs. Goforth is a wealthy American who seems able to murder on her island with impunity. Then, too, she is conspicuous consumption incarnate. She parades an incredible variety of opulent dishes before the Witch at dinner, but throughout the film she eats nothing; she only drinks. She flaunts her luxuries but throws away the simple food for which Flanders is famished.

Mrs. Goforth's aloofness makes her unable to individualize other people. For example, she refers to Flanders as "Manders-Sanders." And she wonders how Blackie "could have a husband named Charles and not call him Charlie." Mrs. Goforth recalls that she once liked to meet people, before they all seemed to become the same person over and over again and I tired of that person." At one point reference is made to a benefit ball for "tycoon or typhoon victims." As so often in the best writing, a malapropism tells a deeper truth through its appearance of error. For Mrs. Goforth is a tycoon who is like a typhoon, a stormy, destructive spirit who presumes to superhuman authority. "What's human and what's inhuman is not for human decision," she tells Blackie. With Flanders and Mrs. Goforth played by coevals, the film emphasizes the power that accrues to class advantage and wealth, and the forces of nature—storm, tide, and ravaging time—that level all men.

Moreover, three myths interweave through the casting of Burton and Taylor. First, she is The Girl Who Had Everything (including a film of that title), whose adult persona is a woman under remarkable stress. Second, there is the Burton myth. He brings to the film a sense of wasted talent that the first choice for the role, Sean Connery, with his persona of James Bond success, would have lacked. Third, there is the legendary romance of Burton and Taylor together, which makes the romantic involvement between Flanders and Goforth seem inevitable and larger than life. Her death before the romance is conventionally consummated is thus all the more saddening. Moreover, the audience knows them to be tempestuous even in their harmonies, larger than law and convention, from their private lives as well as from their movies together (Cleopatra, The Sandpiper, Who's Afraid of Virginia Woolf?, The Taming of the Shrew, Dr. Faustus). At least one of the movie advertisements centered upon this aspect of the stars, with angry headshots that might have come from any of their movies together.

The stars' personae provide Burton's Flanders with a power over Mrs. Goforth that in the play lies in the charac-

ter's youth and otherworldliness. For Burton's presence suggests a hidden strength throughout Flanders's abuse by Mrs.
Goforth. She refuses him drink and food, teases him sexually,
and persistently insults him, but Burton leaves a sense that he
has a hidden power over this woman. Suddenly he asserts
himself:

> *Goforth:*   Do you sit when a woman stands?
>
> *Flanders:*   Sorry. Sit down.

And she does. Burton has tamed his shrew once again.

Less obvious than the casting is the remarkable sound-
track which Losey developed for the film. For example, the
Goforth mansion abounds with sounds of delicate tin-
kling—ice against glasses, objects against surfaces, and Flanders's mobiles in the breeze. These soft sounds suggest the
delicate values by which humanity can distinguish itself from
the rough boom of nature and its tide, the small ways in which
a tycoon can keep from being like a typhoon.

In contrast, we have the loudness of Mrs. Goforth, as she
shouts at her servants, dictates her memoirs through the in-
tercom, and generally slams around violently. In her loudness, she strives for the boom of nature, but she is hopelessly
dwarfed by the tide, shots of which are cut in to undermine
her imperious utterances. Often her violence ends in a tinkle:
when she smashes a drink, or when she throws the x-ray machine, and then Flanders's meal, down to the sea. The sea
seems to reduce her violence to a tinkle and to roar back, as if
fed, or amused at her pretensions.

For the tide represents the forces of nature, beside which
man is insignificant. The characters will die, but the world's
oldest sea will survive. Thus the last shot of Mrs. Goforth's
corpse is imposed upon a shot of the tide. As Flanders says
"Boom" for the last time, her face disappears, leaving the
tide, a huge and violent constant. Losey earlier pointed man's
smallness against nature by cutting from a shot of the tide that
has swallowed Flanders's meal, to a shot of Mrs. Goforth's
bacteria, as seen through the doctor's microscope.

Flanders understands the boom of the sea, because of what he cites as "the humility of my profession" and "the faith of my profession." The sea gave him his vocation, when he found a rich old man who needed help to die. Now he repays the sea by throwing it Mrs. Goforth's diamond ring, to preserve the purity of his mission.

Flanders also serves the natural forces with his art. First, he builds mobiles that will surrender to the movement of the winds and make music with them. Second, he verbalizes the power of the sea when, from time to time, he pronounces the "Boom" himself. With his soft, gentle voice, he invokes and seems to control the uncontrollable forces of nature. His one-word poem is his submission to the tide; the artist controls his material by submitting to its essence.

And there is glory in Flanders's appreciation of the power beyond him. Hence his explication of the word "Boom": "the shock of each moment of still being alive." For Mrs. Goforth, life is impossible to hold, despite (or because of) her power: "Life is all memory except each moment that goes by so quickly you can hardly catch it." But the poet can by his art bring the passing moment under his hold. This is the point that Williams makes in his preface to The Rose Tattoo; art can freeze an instant of life for control and understanding. So too in BOOM, Flanders can serve and control through the humility of his art the tide that dwarfs the utterances of Mrs. Goforth. Flanders quotes from Coleridge's "Kubla Khan" because he too has observed human failures at decreeing pleasure and permanence. In art there is a permanence that life does not afford. So Flanders's art is represented by two books—his volume of poems and his volume that lists the old people whom he has eased into death. Both are records of his creative effect. As an epigraph to the play, Williams quoted four lines from Yeats's "Sailing to Byzantium," where the poet yearns to escape his dying animality, "into the artifice of eternity." Within the play, Flanders practices his artifice with faith and with humility, in his poetry, his mobiles, and his profession of preparing his patrons for death.

The arts are also an important element in Richard Mac-
Donald's brilliant set designs for the film. Of course, "You
can tell a man by the things he owns," as we hear in the hair
oil commercial in Losey's *Eve*. So Mrs. Goforth has a splendid
art collection. Flanders awakens under an inverted Chagall of
time, music, and the flesh. The next scene opens on a huge
Renaissance canvas, from which the camera pans away to
find Mrs. Goforth commanding her servants with the gentleness of a Borgia. Thus the characters are defined by the art
around them. For instance, Flanders's allegorical shading as
the Angel of Death and his personal warmth are both expressed in the Chagall. And Mrs. Goforth's power and dissolution are imaged in the passage from the rich Renaissance canvas to a coarser, grimacing peasant from a
Bosch. In addition, the art reminds us of Mrs. Goforth's edu-
cation and wealth, and points up her failure in human respon-
siveness. She also remains detached from her art, with the
sole exception of a massive hanging wall sculpture, which
seems to embrace her when she prepares to die. This abstract
piece parallels the winds that billowed the curtains in her
room earlier, as Flanders's mobiles and poetry obey the wind
and the tide.

MacDonald also designed a magnificent villa for Mrs.
Goforth. It has huge, naked, white spaces and eerie eye-like
windows gouged out of the deep stone. The villa, like the island over which it looms, is an image of Mrs. Goforth's isolation, hardness, and coldness. Through these vacancies Mrs.
Goforth strides, in Flanders's words, "without reason," drifting as Karen Stone did in the earlier film.

The costuming is as expressive as the sets. Blackie, the
most human character in the film, wears earth-brown sweat-
er and slacks. Mrs. Goforth usually wears white, in her all-
white rooms, as if of a piece with the cold stone walls. Her
Kabuki costume, and the Samurai gown in which she bedecks
Flanders, acknowledge Williams's use of Kabuki-like stage
assistants in the original play, as well as expressing the theat-
ricality and vain artifice in Mrs. Goforth's nature.

Finally one must remark upon the brilliant camera work, what Harold Pinter has described as Losey's "remorseless eye," with its "constant movement, a balance of constant curiosity, almost an anxiety," with "an extraordinary eye for detail."[3] Thus the camera angles change the dwarf into a giant and the villa into a desert. Thus, too, Noël Coward makes what seems to be an elegant entrance, but the camera draws back to reveal him inelegantly carried atop a servant's shoulders. This one movement replays what is such a vital theme in this work, the parasitic nature of people with more power than humanity.

One last example of the film's expressive power may suffice. When Mrs. Goforth turns on a music tape, the camera holds for an inordinately long time on her finger, with its huge diamond ring. One implication is that she turns on the music for the same reason that she flashes her ring—to assert her power. Then, too, for that brief suspension of real time in the shot, it helps to locate the drama in the Burton-Taylor myth, which includes the exchange of opulent diamond gifts. There is also something ominous and portending disaster in the duration of the shot. The ring makes Mrs. Goforth seem vulnerable, for we share her suspicion that Flanders may be a fortune hunter. Finally, Losey cut to the ring from the booming tide, to imply that her fortune is her only defense against the power of nature. And a fragile defense it proves to be, when Flanders removes it and feeds it to the sea.

BOOM was originally titled *Goforth*, but the tide became the central image. The new title alerts us to the significance of the technical effects, for this is a film that speaks to us in filmic ways. There is a fine literary script, but this is the Williams film in which the characteristic resources of film—time, light, sound, color, the physical world of the settings, and the mythic world of the cast—are most fruitfully deployed.

15

Last of the Mobile Hot-shots

(1969)

Sidney Lumet's film is not, properly speaking, an adaptation in the traditional sense. It claims to be "based upon" Tennessee Williams's play, *The Seven Descents of Myrtle* (which was published as *Kingdom of Earth*). By changing the title, Lumet avoids the pretense of presenting Williams's work, so he exempts the film from the criteria of fidelity by which we usually judge an adaptation. In the credits and in the advertisements, however, Lumet acknowledges the source that he refashioned. Predictably, Williams finds the work "perfectly disastrous."[1] Lumet admits that "it wasn't a success," but that he "would rather do incomplete Tennessee Williams than complete-anyone-else."[2] Still, Lumet did not "complete" Williams's play, so much as shift its emphasis from the theme of survival to an anatomy of racism.

The play is set in the decaying Deep South estate of the Ravenstock family on the eve of a flood. Lot Ravenstock is dying of tuberculosis. The farm has been worked by his illegitimate mulatto half-brother Chicken, in return for Lot's contracting to leave him the estate when he dies. Now Lot dreads resigning his elegant mother's home to the vulgar Chicken. So he brings home a wife, Myrtle, whom he met and wed on a television game show. Lot sends Myrtle to get Chicken drunk in order to steal Lot's contract. Instead, Chicken convinces Myrtle that her only hope of surviving the flood rests with him. So Myrtle surrenders to Chicken. Decked in his mother's fancy gowns, Lot descends from his sick room and dies. As the waters approach, Chicken and Myrtle retreat to the roof to survey their flooded empire.

Williams's central theme is survival. Chicken has his name from the way he survives floods by perching with the chickens on the rooftop and drinking chickens' blood. Myrtle is the only survivor of The Mobile Hot-shots, a singing quartet, in which she was known as the Petite Personality Kid. In a stage direction Williams remarks that "She has nothing else to meet the world with but good nature" (p.4). The personable Myrtle and the coarse Chicken are opposites who survive by the force of their character. Lot fails to survive, for instead of character he has only the false pretense to his mother's suspect glory.

The "seven descents" of the original title of the play refer to the varieties of debasement by which Myrtle manages to survive. Four descents are physical—four times she goes down the stairs from her husband's sickroom to attempt to inveigle the dreaded Chicken. Two descents are verbal. First, she "goes down" on Chicken (p.95) when she accepts him as a lover. Secondly, she abandons her faith in the Savior, who "has never let me down." As she says this, "The bright light is now fixed on Chicken" (p.105), her new savior. Myrtle's final descent occurs, paradoxically, when she climbs onto the roof with Chicken. In order to survive, the southern belle abandons all her principles, including fidelity, faith, and her horror of miscegenation. Thus Myrtle exemplifies Chicken's observation: "What people have to do, they always do" (p.104).

As additional emblems of the survival instinct, both men are cunning and relentless in their attempts to retain the estate. Lot's justification is based upon his image of the family's glorious past. He dreams about restoring the estate to its antebellum majesty: "What a beautiful way of life we used to have ... what a natural way." But Chicken's claim is rooted in the immediate reality: slavery is dead, he worked the place, so it should be his. In the contrast between the fragile, nostal-

gic Lot and the brutish, indomitable Chicken, Williams returns to the opposition between Blanche DuBois and Stanley
Kowalski. In this work, however, the sensitive creature dies
in a paroxysm of malice and delusions of lost glory. This time
our sympathy is with the survivor.

The three characters also provide different variations
upon conventional religion. The faith by which Lot lives, for
instance, is his idolizing of his dead mother and the elegant
earlier age which she represents. He even dies trying to assume her image, in what Williams describes as "the sexless
passion of the transvestite" (p.108). This contrasts to Chick-
en's religion of lust and "personal satisfaction": "You can't
haul down your spiritual gates if you don't have any in you."
A preacher fails to instill a sense of shame in him. Nothing in
"this kingdom of earth" can compare with "what's able to
happen between a man and a woman, just that thing, nothing
more, is perfect" (pp.105-7).

Myrtle, like Chicken, is a vulgar, hearty survivor; so her
creed is closer to his than to Lot's. Though she pays lip service
to her religion, she readily throws in her lot with Chicken, so
to speak, to extend her life on earth. (Her baptism has left her
with a fear of drowning.) For both, life is for living and loving; survival is man's basic aim and pleasure his greatest re-
ward.

In his film, Lumet omits Chicken's religious statement altogether. The name of Lot Ravenstock is changed to Jeb Stuart
Thorington, a name without biblical associations. The only religious element in the film is the barely audible country and
western song, "Jesus Was a Soul Man," that plays over the
opening titles. This song works less as a religious statement
than to set up a movement from the ersatz "soul" music at the
beginning to the wilder, genuine, black soul music at the end,
when Chicken has come into his kingdom. Lumet shows the
wedding ceremony on Rube Benedict's television show, before an altar of prize electrical appliances. But in this scene,
the emphasis is on the grossness of media commercialism. So

extravagant is the satire that no sense of (even lost) sacra-
ment survives in the wedding. Lumet seems deliberately to
have omitted the religious aspect of Williams's play.

Instead, Lumet expanded the social theme of racism. He
cast a black actor, Robert Hooks, as Chicken, the man sus-
pected of having black blood in his lineage. Williams introduces Chicken as "a strange-looking young man ... remarkably good-looking with his very light eyes, [and] darker-than-
olive skin" (p.3). When José Quintero directed the original
production of the play (which opened in New York on March
27, 1968, with Estelle Parsons and Brian Bedford), a white actor, Harry Guardino, played Chicken. There was something of
a shock to the audience—and to Myrtle—when Chicken ad-
mitted he was considered a Negro. Lumet's casting costs the
play this surprise and the character his ambiguity. Worse, it
disrupts the balance of Williams's play, for it makes the central tension that between black man and white, where in the
play there are more subtle distinctions pertaining to survival
and faith. With a black Chicken, his claim to our approval becomes a matter of racial equality, not Williams's assertion of
the supremacy of man's physical nature over spiritual ab-
stractions.

But we must give Lumet his due. He wholeheartedly
reshaped the material to support the redirection he chose to
give the play. He has Chicken reveal that it was Jeb's mother,
not his father, whose transgression brought him to life. The
father bore the shame to preserve his wife's honor. The film
makes the mother's honor a more spectacular lie than it is
in the play, where she is only unfaithful with the fruitseller.
Her elegance is a hypocrisy; she refused to let the black maid
touch her crystal chandelier, but she had a son by the black
handyman.

Lumet also develops a series of flashbacks that delineate
Jeb's racist schizophrenia. For example, Jeb idealizes his
mother but retains memories of his black nanny's nipple. The
idea that he and Chicken had the same mother is too much for

him to bear. Further, he remembers the sexual camaraderie he and Chicken once enjoyed; now Jeb's potency is blocked by his image of himself as weak, pale, cowering against the wall, while Chicken has sex with a beautiful blonde. Jeb is incapacitated by this image of himself (in this series of flashbacks), rather than by any threat Chicken poses. Lumet's dramatization of the racist's paranoia is consistent and subtle.

Lumet draws some comedy from actor Hooks's blackness. For instance, it takes a powerful effort of Myrtle's will to deny the rumor that Chicken may have some black blood, when she is faced by a clearly black Chicken. This is a comic parallel to the tragically blinkered vision by which Jeb sustains his fantasies. Chicken's claims to be "dark complected" add a new element of understatement to his character. "I can see color," he says drily of Myrtle's snapshot—a line of stronger irony when spoken by a Negro than by a possible mulatto. Finally, Lumet and screenwriter Gore Vidal give Myrtle a number of songs about watermelons and "nigguhs" by which she tries to ingratiate herself with Chicken. This comedy expresses Myrtle's insensitivity and the grounds for Chicken's indignation.

Lumet's casting of Hooks is defensible because of the ironic undertones it gives the role. The casting of James Coburn as the impotent, deluded Jeb is also shrewd. It undercuts Coburn's film persona as the able and attractive man of amoral integrity (*Flint, Duffy, Waterhole No. 3*). Jeb's first appearance in the film is as a helpless drunk thrown out of a bar. In the film he is allowed none of the initial sympathy he has in the play, because Coburn's star presence could be assumed to carry its own appeal. Lynn Redgrave is another well-cast persona. As an English actress playing a Williams Southern belle, she seems to function as a gauche, comic parody of Vivien Leigh's Blanche and Karen Stone. Moreover, since her roles in *The Girl With Green Eyes* and *Georgy Girl*, Redgrave has developed the image of a simple, vulgar, but extremely warm and good-natured character (to be expressed *in extremis* as *The Happy Hooker);* these qualities enhance her performance as Myrtle, her voice imparting a shrill edge to her hardiness.

All in all, the film is a provocative minor work by a major American director. It may be illuminating to compare the film to the specifics of the original. For example, Williams ended the play with the spirited couple retreating to the rooftop, but Lumet takes them further. He shows them on the roof, huddled under Chicken's chicken-yellow raincape, shrinking to a yellow speck as the camera draws back for a long view of the flooded landscape. Typically, Lumet refers his characters to their physical and social settings. His characters are emblems of a time in American social history, more specifically than Williams's were. Indeed, one might suggest that the film is more deeply related to Lumet's *The Pawnbroker* (1963), both in theme and in technique, than it is to Williams's play, which is nowhere as topical as the film. But in this one respect Lumet's film remains a model of adaptation: it was honest enough to change its name when it changed its nature.

Conclusion

The history of Tennessee Williams's films chronicles the maturing of the American screen. In the beginning there was the artifically sweetened *The Glass Menagerie*. But with *A Streetcar Named Desire* the concept of movies for mature adults—dormant in America since Ernst Lubitsch and Josef von Sternberg—was revived. Though this was followed by the domestication of *The Rose Tattoo* and the scandal over *Baby Doll*, the American cinema grew to be able to deal with William's work. Eventually there was *Suddenly Last Summer* and *BOOM*.

Before *A Streetcar Named Desire* appeared, even a controversial film, deliberately addressed to the thinking audience, was expected to be suitable viewing for children. There were unwritten limits to the kind of controversy that could be brought to the public screen—and to its degree of complexity. At best, a "controversial" film would draw attention to what was already recognized as a social problem. Moreover, it would take the widely accepted position. Thus *The Ox Bow Incident* (1943) proves that lynching is wrong, but does so in practical, not moral, terms; its point is that the wrong man may be hung, not that lynching is wrong in itself.

Today we are often struck by the blandness of films that were considered controversial in their time: *Lost Weekend* (1945), *Crossfire* (1947), *Sunset Boulevard* (1950), *All About Eve* (1950), *Intruder in the Dust* (1950), *The Big Carnival*

137

(1951). If a film strayed from the acceptable position on an acceptable problem, it would be denied an audience— Chaplin's *Monsieur Verdoux (1947) and A King in New York* (1957) are cases in point. (Often a work was softened to bring its controversial elements into line. Thus when Richard Brooks's novel, *The Brick Foxhole,* was filmed as *Crossfire,* the victim was changed from a homosexual to a Jew.) It was into this nervous, fastidious atmosphere that the plays of Tennessee Williams came to be filmed.

The prestige of Williams's theater work eased his acceptance in film. *The Glass Menagerie* immediately established him as a major dramatist, and very early in his career there was a public demand for film versions of his plays. Williams's name was more prominent in the film advertisements than the director's, and sometimes equal to the stars'. As he accumulated theatrical successes, the sensational themes that he treated became more respectable subject matter for other dramatists—and finally, film makers. So the Williams films, bolstered by their theatrical prestige, enabled American film makers to treat other adult, even sensational, themes. After Williams, others could deal with rape, the dilemma of a child bride, the stultifying faith of a Catholic widow, homosexuality, the consuming but liberating power of the imagination, the religious spirit in sexuality, a widow's moral and sensual resurrection, and the magnificence of human perseverance in the face of despair. These are far more complex concerns than the social problems to which the earlier "serious movie" was restricted: alcoholism, prejudice, and the corruption of Hollywood or the press.

There may seem to be a sexual bias to the liberalization that Williams helped to bring to the American cinema. But he was a political force as well, by virtue of the fact that he was a revolutionary both in the technique and in the themes of his work. For Williams challenged our accepted sense of what man and society are and what art may do. Jean-Luc Godard seems to acknowledge this in his film *La Chinoise* (1967).

There Williams's name is among those that a young revolutionary writes upon a blackboard as heroes who have advanced world freedom and equality. He erases some of the names, but Williams's remains.

Williams's most explicitly political work was done in collaboration with Elia Kazan. Had they continued to work together, particularly on *Period of Adjustment*, Williams's political disposition might have emerged more clearly. Nevertheless, his films still present a political force.

In addition to the radical effect Williams had in maturing the subject matter of American film, the adaptations of his plays provided the first wide exposure to the techniques of the Actors Studio (The Method) and to its leading students. American film acting was revolutionized by the motive-centered naturalism of the Studio-Williams stars: Marlon Brando, Kim Hunter, Karl Malden, Jo Van Fleet, Geraldine Page, Eli Wallach, Paul Newman, Joanne Woodward, Maureen Stapleton, Shirley Knight, Rip Torn. Into the 1970s, some of the best film performances—by Dustin Hoffman, Al Pacino, Ellen Burstyn, Robert De Niro, Marlon Brando—derive from the Studio technique and style. So the Williams films were an important force in accustoming the audience to the inner-directed and realistic acting style that replaced the theatrical rhetoric of the films of the 1950s.

Within the industry, Williams seems to have been an important force in establishing the importance of the writer in the Hollywood system. Because of his own fame and the commercial power of his plays, Williams was treated better than writers commonly were. For example, he sold screen rights to his plays for remarkable fees, sometimes including a percentage of the profits. Moreover, for the film of *The Roman Spring of Mrs. Stone*, Williams was granted approval rights on the director, the script, the two leads, and the final print. Even the number of times that Williams worked on the screenplay himself or attended the shooting is remarkable in an industry that tends to forget the writer—and often even his text—as filming nears. Thus Williams set a salutary example for the more assertive generation of screenwriters that followed.

An analogous claim might be made in aesthetic terms. That is, Williams kept alive the sense that a film is to be heard as well as seen, that there is delight in the precise and evocative wording of an idea or a feeling, however rich cinema might be visually. In the Williams films as a whole there is a remarkable use of language, both in poetic flourish and in irony. Often his poetry is powerful enough for the play to survive its abuse—*The Glass Menagerie, Sweet Bird of Youth*—or its redirection, as in *Last of the Mobile Hot-shots*. Other films, particularly *Suddenly Last Summer, The Fugitive Kind*, and *BOOM*—are a delight to listen to. They remind us that film, despite its visual and temporal impact, remains a medium with a powerful verbal potential. Indeed if *This Property Is Condemned* does not at first seem like a Williams film it is because it lacks his verbal richness, once the action leaves Willie's chat on the railroad tracks.

But having made these claims for Williams's filmed work I must add a regretful reservation about the extent of his commitment to film. For all the success of his adaptations, Williams does not seem to have taken the medium as seriously as he might have done.

For one thing, his only original screenplay to have been realized, *Baby Doll*, lacks the intensity and ambition that characterizes his theater work of the time. Moreover, he seems too often to have accepted the compromises of the industry and too often countenanced the release of an inadequate adaptation (*The Rose Tattoo, Period of Adustment*). Conversely, he has often underestimated the fidelity of some treatments of his work—most notably, *Suddenly Last Summer* and *The Night of the Iguana*—perhaps betraying a failure to have explored fully enough the implications of how film works.

Granted, there has been a rich exchange between Williams's stage and his film experience. But he has never been the kind of film student that such writers as, say, Harold Pinter and Alain Robbe-Grillet have been. Rather, Williams was a fan—an enthusiast, but merely a fan. Hence his friend Gilbert Maxwell's confession that "To this day, Tenn and I are childishly ardent movie fans. We go to pictures together and always sit in the loge where we can whisper and laugh without disturbing too many people, or being summarily ejected for becoming helpless with glee when a film turns out to be unintentionally funny."[1] Given Williams's genius, one might wish that he had explored the film medium with a more serious devotion.

But for the most part, Williams was well served by his directors, all of whom were experienced both in theater and in film, all of whom were more than "childishly ardent" fans. As a result, Williams's plays generally weathered their filming rather well, though in some cases they have suffered from the decorum of their day. But wholesale misrepresentations are rare (*The Glass Menagerie, Sweet Bird of Youth*). More often we find lapses in discretion or errors in emphasis, as in *Cat on a Hot Tin Roof* and *Period of Adjustment*, where the problems of interpretation might just as likely have arisen in a stage production. Generally speaking, one finds a deep respect for Williams in the work. In *This Property Is Condemned* the film's additions seem to assume a general knowledge of Williams's other works, suggesting that the playwright has been absorbed into the basic culture of the land for ready quotation. But even someone coming fresh to Williams through his films alone would find fair access to his primary concerns—man's cruelty, his mendacity, the tragic clash between the imaginative soul and the creature of brutish realism—and a sense of his technical mastery, his strong characterization, his flair for dramatic incident, and his evocative language.

Of course, there are infidelities large and small in the film adaptations, but there are also hosts of creative liberties, which distinguish the solid, sensitive productions of *A Streetcar Named Desire*, *The Fugitive Kind*, *Summer and Smoke*,

and *The Roman Spring of Mrs. Stone.* Perhaps best of all are
those cases in which the original seems to have sparked the
film director's intelligence, and a lively, different work
emerges.

Such is the case in the film version of *This Property Is
Condemned* but most strikingly in both *The Night of the
Iguana* and *BOOM.* These are the best of the Williams adaptations because in both there is the energy and freedom of
original creativity. They work so well as art that reservations
about their specific relationship to the original work seem
like caviling. Clearly directors John Huston and Joseph Losey
responded so intensely to Williams's plays that they needed
some latitude to develop their responses. The result in each
case was a film that combined the essential elements of Williams's original with the film maker's profound sense of his
craft and of his performers' expressiveness. The author is
well served by the reflective liberties that these films take
with his work.

Notes

Unless otherwise noted, all quotations are from film prints in the collection of the Library of Congress, Washington, D.C.

Introduction

[1] Quoted in Gilbert Maxwell, *Tennessee Williams and Friends* (Cleveland: World Publishing, 1965), p. xii.
[2] Quoted in Gordon Gow, *Hollywood in the Fifties* (New York: Barnes, 1971), p.50.
[3] Tennessee Williams, *Memoirs* (New York: Doubleday, 1975), p.173.
[4] Compare André Bazin, *What Is Cinema?* Vol. I (Berkeley and Los Angeles: University of California Press, 1967), pp.76-124.

1. The Glass Menagerie

[1] Hugh MacMullan, "Translating *The Glass Menagerie* to Film," *Hollywood Quarterly*, V (1950-51), pp. 14-32.
[2] John Calendo, Tennessee Talks to John Calendo," *Interview*, April, 1973, p.44.

2. A Streetcar Named Desire

[1] Michel Delahaye, "A Natural Phenomenon," *Cahiers du Cinema in English*, No. 9, March, 1967, p.14.

2 Elia Kazan, "Notebook for *A Streetcar Named Desire*," in Toby Cole and Helen Krich Chinoy, eds., *Directors on Directing* (London: Peter Owen and Vision Press, 1964), pp.364-79.

3 Published in George P. Garrett, O.B. Hardison Jr., and Jane R. Gelfman, eds., *Film Scripts One* (New York: Appleton-Century-Crofts, 1971), p.333.

4 Compare Murray Schumach, "A Streetcar Named Milestone," in *The Face on the Cutting Room Floor* (New York: William Morrow; Da Capo paperback, 1975), pp. 71-79.

5 Michel Ciment, *Kazan on Kazan* (London: Secker and Warburg, 1973), pp.68-69.

6 "In the Script: *A Streetcar Named Desire*," *Sight and Sound*, April-June, 1952, pp.173-75.

7 Williams's caption to a still, Illus. 102, in *Memoirs*.

3. *The Rose Tattoo*

1 Tennessee Williams, *Memoirs*, p.161.

2 Compare John Howard Reid, "Portraying Life With Dignity," *Films and Filming*, March 1962, pp. 19-20.

4. *Baby Doll*

1 Compare Murray Schumach, *The Face on the Cutting Room Floor*, pp.95-96, 202.

2 For example, Henry Hewes, "The Boundaries of Tennessee," *Saturday Review*, December 29, 1956, pp.23-24; Arthur Knight, "The Williams-Kazan Axis," *Saturday Review*, December 29, 1956, pp.22-23; Nathan Scott, Jr., "Movies: The *Baby Doll* Furor," *The Christian Century*, January 23, 1957, pp.110-12.

3 Mike Steen, *A Look At Tennessee Williams* (New York: Hawthorn Books, 1969), p.4.

4 See Boris Kaufman, "Filming *Baby Doll*," *American Cinematographer*, February, 1957, pp. 92-93, 106-7.

5. *Cat on a Hot Tin Roof*

1 For example, Peter Baker, "*Cat on a Hot Tin Roof*," *Films and Film-*

ing, November, 1958, p.21; Rod McManigal, *"Cat on a Hot Tin Roof,"* *Sight and Sound,* Winter, 1958-59, p.36.

2 Tennessee Williams, "Let It All Hang Out," *New York Times,* March 4, 1973. Compare *Memoirs,* pp.168-69.

3 "She giggles with a hand fluttering at her throat and her breast and her long throat arched" (Williams's stage directions, p.114).

4 Bernard Kantor, Irwin Blacker, and Anne Kramer, *Directors at Work* (New York: Funk and Wagnalls, 1970), p.26.

5 See Williams's Note of Explanation, pp.198-99.

6 Peter Baker, *"Cat on a Hot Tin Roof."* McManigal agrees.

7 Edward Murray, *The Cinematic Imagination* (New York: Frederick Ungar, 1972), p. 60.

8 In Arthur Waters, "Tennessee Williams: Ten Years Later," *Theater Arts,* July, 1955, p.73.

9 Rip Torn suggests this reading in Mike Steen, *A Look at Tennessee Williams,* p.211.

10 "Tennessee Williams: Interview," *Playboy,* April, 1973, p.82.

11 Quoted in John Gruen, *Close-Up* (New York: Viking, 1968) p.93. Richard Brooks claims that Williams was consulted throughout the production ("Richard Brooks," *Movie,* No. 12, Spring, 1965, p.8).

6. *Suddenly Last Summer*

1 John Calendo, "Tennessee Talks to John Calendo," *Interview,* April, 1973, p.44.

2 See Hollis Alpert, "In a Messel Garden," *Films and Filming,* January, 1960, pp.8, 32.

3 Quoted in Gary Carey, *More About "All About Eve"* (New York: Random House, 1972; Bantam paperback, 1974), p.56. Compare Joseph Mankiewicz, "Measure for Measure," *Cahiers du Cinema in English,* No. 8, February, 1967, p.35.

4 See Carey, pp. 94-95.

5 Quoted in Derek Conrad, "Putting on the Style," *Films and Filming,* January, 1960, p.9.

7. *The Fugitive Kind*

1 Peter Bogdanovich, "An Interview with Sidney Lumet," *Film Quarterly,* Winter, 1960, p.18.

[2] Stephen Farber, "Lumet in '69," *Sight and Sound*, Autumn, 1969, pp.190-95.

8. *Summer and Smoke*

[1] Darrin Scot, "The Lang Touch," *American Cinematographer*, December, 1961, pp.732-33, 746, 748.

9. *The Roman Spring of Mrs. Stone*

[1] José Quintero, *If You Don't Dance They Beat You* (Boston: Little Brown, 1974), p.265.

10. *Sweet Bird of Youth*

[1] W.J. Weatherby, "Lonely in Uptown New York," *Manchester Guardian Weekly*, July 23, 1959, p.14.
[2] Richard Brooks, "Richard Brooks," *Movie*, No. 12, Spring, 1965, p.8.
[3] Tennessee Williams: "Interview," *Playboy*, April, 1973, p.82.

11. *Period of Adjustment*

[1] Quoted in Lewis Funke and John E. Booth, "Williams on Williams," *Theater Arts*, January, 1962, p.72.
[2] Tennessee Williams, "Prelude to a Comedy," *New York Times*, November 6, 1960, Section D, p.1.

12. *The Night of the Iguana*

[1] Quoted in Lewis Funke and John E. Booth, "Williams on Williams," *Theater Arts*, January, 1962, p.72.
[2] Quoted in John Calendo, "Tennessee Talks to John Calendo," *Interview*, April, 1973, p.44.
[3] Robert Gessner, *The Moving Image* (New York: E.P. Dutton, 1968), pp.224-27.

4 Compare Gene Phillipps, "Talking with John Huston," *Film Comment*, May-June, 1973, pp.15-19; Tom Reck, "Huston Meets the Eye," Same issue, pp. 6-11.

13. *This Property Is Condemned*

1 Raymond Durgnat, *"This Property Is Condemned," Films and Filming*, November, 1966, pp.6-8.
2 Patricia Erens, "Sidney Pollack: The Way We Are," *Film Comment*, September-October, 1975, pp. 24-29.
3 Tennessee Williams, *Memoirs*, note to Illus. 136.

14. *BOOM*

1 Tennessee Williams, *Memoirs*, p. 198; compare pp.183, 200.
2 Quoted in John Calendo, "Tennessee Talks to John Calendo," *Interview*, April, 1973, p.28.
3 Quoted from a program on Losey in the Thames TV series, "Movie Men," telecast on July 28, 1970.

15. *Last of the Mobile Hot-shots*

1 Rex Reed, *People Are Crazy Here* (New York: Delacorte Press; Dell paperback, 1975), p.223.
2 Quoted in Gordon Gow, "What's Real? What's True?" *Films and Filming*, May, 1975, p.16. Compare Lumet in Fred Baker, ed., *Movie People* (New York: Douglas Book Corporation, 1972), p.44.

Conclusion

1 Gilbert Maxwell, *Tennessee Williams and Friends* (Cleveland: World Publishing Co., 1965), p. xii.

Filmography

The Glass Menagerie (1950). *Director:* Irving Rapper. *Producers:* Jerry Wald, Charles K. Feldman. *Screenplay: adapted by* Tennessee Williams *and* Peter Berneis. *Photography:* Robert Burks. *Music:* Max Steiner. *Art Director:* Robert Haas. Warner Brothers. 107 minutes.

Jane Wyman *(Laura).* Kirk Douglas *(Jim).* Gertrude Lawrence *(Amanda).* Arthur Kennedy *(Tom).* Ralph Sanford *(Mendoza).* Ann Tyrrell *(Clerk).* John Compton *(Young man).* Gertrude Graner *(Teacher).* Sara Edwards *(Mrs. Miller).* Louise Lorrimer *(Miss Porter).* Chris Alcaide *(Eddie).* Perdita Chandler *(Girl).*

A Streetcar Named Desire (1951). *Director:* Elia Kazan. *Producer:* Charles K. Feldman. *Screenplay:* Elia Kazan, *adaptation by* Oscar Saul. *Photography:* Harry Stradling. *Music:* Alex North. *Art Director:* Richard Day. Warner Brothers. 125 minutes.

Vivien Leigh *(Blanche).* Marlon Brando *(Stanley).* Kim Hunter *(Stella).* Karl Malden *(Mitch).* Rudy Bond *(Steve).* Nick Dennis *(Pablo).* Peg Hillias *(Eunice).* Wright King *(Collector).* Richard Garrick *(Doctor).* Anne Dere *(Matron).* Edna Thomas *(Mexican woman).* Chester Jones *(Street vendor).* Marietta Canty *(Negro woman).* Lyle Latell *(Policeman).* Mel Archer *(Foreman).* Charles Wagenheim, Maxie Thrower *(passersby).* Mickey Kuhn *(Sailor).*

The Rose Tattoo (1955). *Director:* Daniel Mann. *Producer:* Hal Wallis. *Screenplay:* Tennessee Williams, *adapted by* Hal Kanter. *Photography:* James Wong Howe. *Music:* Alex North. *Special photo-*

graphic effects: John P. Fulton, *Art Directors:* Hal Pereira, Tambia Larsen. *Assistant Director:* Richard McWhorter. Vista Vision. Paramount. 117 minutes.

> Anna Magnani *(Serafina)*. Burt Lancaster *(Alvaro)*. Marisa Pavan *(Rosa)*. Ben Cooper *(Jack Hunter)*. Virginia Grey *(Estelle)*. Jo Van Fleet *(Bessie)*. Sandro Giglio *(Father De Leo)*. Mimi Aguglia *(Assunta)*. Florence Sundstrom *(Flora)*. Dorrit Kelton *(Teacher)*. Rossana san Marco *(Peppina)*. Augusta Merighi *(Giuseppina)*. Rosa Rey *(Mariella)*. Zolya Talma *(Miss Mangiacavallo)*. George Humbert *(Papa Mangiacavallo)*. Margherita Pasquero *(Grandma Mangiacavallo)*. May Lee *(Tattooist)*. Lewis Charles *(Taxi-driver)*.

Baby Doll (1956). *Director/Producer:* Elia Kazan. *Screenplay and story:* Tennessee Williams. *Photography:* Boris Kaufman. *Music:* Kenyon Hopkins. *Art Director:* Richard Sylbert. *Assistant Director:* Charles H. Maguire. A Newtown Production. Warner Brothers. 114 minutes.

> Karl Malden *(Archie)*. Carroll Baker *(Baby Doll)*. Eli Wallach *(Silva Vacarro)*. Mildred Dunnock *(Aunt Rose)*. Lonny Chapman *(Rock)*. Eades Hogue *(Town marshal)*. Noah Williamson *(Deputy)*. Rip Torn *(Dentist)*. John Dudley *(Doc)*, and the people of Benoit, Mississippi.

Cat on a Hot Tin Roof (1958). *Director:* Richard Brooks. *Producer:* Lawrence Weingarten. *Screenplay:* Richard Brooks *and* James Poe. *Photography:* William Daniels. *Art Directors:*William A. Horning, Urie McCleary. *Assistant Director:* William Shanks. An Avon Production in Metrocolor. MGM. 108 minutes.

> Elizabeth Taylor *(Maggie)*. Paul Newman *(Brick)*. Burl Ives *(Big Daddy)*. Jack Carson *(Gooper)*. Judith Anderson *(Big Mama)*. Madeleine Sherwood *(Mae)*. Larry Gates *(Dr. Bough)*. Vaughn Taylor *(Deacon Davis)*. Brian Corcoran, Hugh Corcoran, Patty Ann Garrity, Deborah Miller *("No-neck monsters")*.

Suddenly Last Summer (1959). *Director:* Joseph L. Mankiewicz. *Producer:* Sam Spiegel. *Screenplay:* Gore Vidal *and* Tennessee Williams. *Production designed by* Oliver Messel. *Photography:* Jack Hildyard. *Music:* Buxton Orr, Malcolm Arnold. *Art Director:* William Kellner. *Photographic Effects:* Tom Howard. Columbia Pictures. 114 minutes.

Elizabeth Taylor *(Catherine Holly).* Katherine Hepburn *(Mrs. Venable).* Montgomery Clift *(Dr. Cukrowicz).* Albert Dekker *(Dr. Hockstader).* Mercedes McCambridge *(Mrs. Holly).* Gary Raymond *(George Holly).* Mavis Villiers *(Miss Foxhill).* Patricia Marmont *(Nurse Benson).* Joan Young *(Sister Felicity).* Maria Britneva *(Lucy).* Sheila Roberts *(Dr. Hockstader's secretary).* David Cameron *(Interne).*

The Fugitive Kind (1960). *Director:* Sidney Lumet. *Producers:* Martin Jurow, Richard A. Shepherd. *Screenplay:* Tennessee Williams and Meade Roberts. *Photography:* Boris Kaufman. *Art Director:* Richard Sylbert. *Music:* Kenyon Hopkins. *Song* ("Blanket Roll Blues"): *Music by Kenyon Hopkins, lyrics by Tennessee Williams. Assistant Director:* Charles H. Maguire. A Jurow-Shepherd-Pennebaker Production. United Artists. 135 minutes.

Marlon Brando *(Val Xavier).* Anna Magnani *(Lady).* Joanne Woodward *(Carol).* Maureen Stapleton *(Vee Talbott).* Victor Jory *(Jabe Torrance).* R.G. Armstrong *(Sheriff Talbott).* Emory Richardson *(Uncle Pleasant).* Sally Gracie *(Dolly Hamma).* Lucille Benson *(Beulah Binnings).* John Baragrey *(David Cutrere).* Ben Yaffee *(Dog Hamma).* Joe Brown, Jr. *(Pee Wee Binnings).* Virginia Chew *(Nurse Porter).* Frank Borgman *(Gas station attendant).* Janice Mars *(Attendant's wife).* Debbie Lynch *(Lonely girl).*

Summer and Smoke (1961). *Director:* Peter Glenville. *Producer:* Hal Wallis. *Screenplay:* James Poe and Meade Roberts. *Photography:* Charles Lang, Jr. *Music:* Elmer Bernstein. *Art Directors:* Walter Tyler, Hal Pereira. *Assistant Directors:* D. Michael Moore, James Rosenberger.

Laurence Harvey *(John Buchanan).* Geraldine Page *(Alma Winemiller).* Rita Moreno *(Rosa).* Una Merkel *(Mrs. Winemiller).* John McIntyre *(Dr. Buchanan).* Malcolm Atterbury (Rev. Winemiller). Pamela Tiffen *(Nellie),* Casey Adams *(Rog-*

er *Doremus*). Thomas Gomez *(Zacharias)*. Earl Holliman *(Archie Kramer)*. Lee Patrick *(Mrs. Ewell)*.

The Roman Spring of Mrs. Stone (1961). *Director:* José Quintero. *Producer:* Louis de Rochemont. *Screenplay:* Gavin Lambert. *Photography:* Harry Waxman. *Music:* Richard Addinsell. *Additional Writing:* Jan Read. *Art Director:* Herbert Smith. *Associate Producer:* Lothar Wolff. *Assistant Director:* Peter Yates. *Production designed* by Roger Furse. *Song* ("Che Noia L'Amor"): Paddy Roberts. A Seven Arts Presentation in Technicolor. Warner Brothers. 104 minutes.

> Vivien Leigh *(Karen Stone)*. Warren Beatty *(Paolo)*. Coral Browne *(Meg)*. Jill St. John *(Barbara)*. Jeremy Spenser *(Young man)*. Stella Bonheur *(Mrs. Jamison Walker)*. Josephine Brown *(Lucia)*. Peter Dyneley *(L. Greener)*. Carl Jaffe *(Baron)*. Harold Kasket *(Tailor)*. Viola Keats *(Julia)*. Cleo Laine *(Singer)*. Bessie Love *(Bunny)*. Elspeth March *(Mrs. Barrow)*. Henry McCarthy *(Kennedy)*. Warren Mitchell *(Giorgio)*. John Phillips *(Tom Stone)*. Paul Stassimo *(Barber)*. Ernest Thesiger *(Stefano)*. Mavis Villiers *(Mrs. Coogan)*. Thelma D'Aguir *(Mita)*. Jean Marsh *(Amanda)*. Lotte Lenya *(Contessa)*.

Sweet Bird of Youth (1962). *Director:* Richard Brooks. *Producer:* Pandro S. Berman. *Screenplay:* Richard Brooks. *Photography:* Milton Krasner. *Music:* Harold Gelman. *Art Directors:* George W. Davis, Urie McCleary. *Associate Producer:* Kathryn Hereford. *Assistant Director:* Hank Moonjean. Cinemascope and Metrocolor. MGM. 120 minutes.

> Paul Newman *(Chance Wayne)*. Geraldine Page *(Alexandra Del Lago)*. Shirley Knight *(Heavenly)*. Ed Begley *(Boss Finley)*. Rip Torn *(Thomas Finley)*. Mildred Dunnock *(Aunt Nonnie)*. Madeleine Sherwood *(Miss Lucy)*. Philip Abbott *(Dr. George Scudder)*. Corey Allen *(Scotty)*. Barny Cahill *(Bud)*. Dub Taylor *(Dan Hatcher)*. James Douglas *(Leroy)*. Barry Atwater *(Ben Jackson)*. Charles Arnt *(Mayor Hendricks)*. Dorothy Konrad *(Mrs. Norris)*. James Chandler *(Prof. Smith)*. Mike Steen *(Deputy)*. Kelly Thordsen *(Sheriff Clark)*.

Period of Adjustment (1962). *Director:* George Roy Hill. *Producer:* Lawrence Weingarten. *Screenplay:* Isobel Lennart. *Photography:*

Paul C. Vogel. *Music:* Lyn Murray. *Art Directors:* George W. Davis, Edward Carfagno. *Assistant Director:* Al Jennings. Panavision. MGM. 112 minutes.

Tony Franciosa *(Ralph Bates)*. Jane Fonda *(Isabel Haverstick)*. Jim Hutton *(George Haverstick)*. Lois Nettleton *(Dorothea Bates)*. John McGiver *(Stewart McGillicuddy)*. Mabel Albertson *(Mrs. McGillicuddy)*. Jack Albertson *(Desk sergeant)*.

The Night of the Iguana (1964). *Director:* John Huston. *Producer:* Ray Stark. *Screenplay:* Anthony Veiller, John Huston. *Photography:* Gabriel Figueroa. *Art Director:* Stephen Grimes. *Music:* Benjamin Frankel. *Assistant Director:* Tom Shaw. A John Huston-Ray Stark Production presented by MGM and Seven Arts. 125 minutes.

Richard Burton *(Rev. T.L. Shannon)*. Ava Gardner *(Maxine Faulk)*. Deborah Kerr *(Hannah Jelkes)*. Sue Lyon *(Charlotte Goodall)*. James Ward *(Hank Prosen)*. Grayson Hall *(Judith Fellowes)*. Cyril Delevanti *(Nonno)*. Mary Boylan *(Miss Peebles)*. Gladys Hill *(Miss Dexter)*. Billie Matticks *(Miss Throxton)*. C.G. Kim *(Chang)*. Roberto Leyva *(Pedro)*. Fildemar Duran *(Pepe)*. Eloise Hardt, Betty Proctor, Dorothy Vance, Liz Rubey, Bernice Starr, Barbara Joyce *(Teachers)*.

This Property Is Condemned (1966). *Director:* Sidney Pollack. *Producer:* John Houseman. *Screenplay:* Francis Ford Coppola, Fred Coe, Edith Sommer. *Photogtaphy:* James Wong Howe. *Music:* Kenyon Hopkins. *Songs:* Jay Livingston, Ray Evans, Sam Coslow, W. Franke Harling, Arthur Johnston, Mildred J. *and* Patty S. Hill. *Art Directors:* Hal Pereira, Stephen Grimes, Phil Jeffries. *Assistant Director:* Eddie Saeta. Presented in Technicolor by Seven Arts and Ray Stark. 110 minutes.

Natalie Wood *(Alva Starr)*. Robert Redford *(Owen Legate)*. Charles Bronson *(J.J. Nichols)*. Kate Reid *(Hazel Starr)*, Mary Badham *(Willie Starr)*. Alan Baxter *(Knopke)*. Robert Blake *(Sidney)*. John Harding *(Johnson)*. Dabney Coleman *(Salesman)*. Ray Hemphill *(Jimmy Bell)*. Brett Pearson *(Charlie Steinkamp)*. Jon Provost *(Tom)*. Quentin Sondergaard *(Hank)*. Mike Steen *(Max)*. Bruce Watson *(Lindsay Tate)*. Bob Random *(Tiny)*.

BOOM (1968). *Director:* Joseph Losey. *Producers:* John Heyman, Norman Priggen. *Screenplay:* Tennessee Williams. *Photography:* Douglas Slocombe. *Music:* John Barry. *Sitar music:* Nazirali Jairazbhoy, Viram Jasani. *Song:* Don Black, John Dankworth. *Art Director:* Richard MacDonald. *Associate Producer:* Lester Persky. *Assistant Director:* Carlo Lastricati. Limites/World Film Services Limited Production in Technicolor. Universal. 110 minutes.

> Elizabeth Taylor *(Flora Goforth)*. Richard Burton *(Chris Flanders)*. Noël Coward *(The Witch of Capri)*. Joanna Shimkus *(Miss Black)*. Michael Dunn *(Rudy)*. Romolo Valli *(Dr. Lullo)*. Fernando Piazza *(Etti)*. Veronica Wells *(Simonetta)*. Claudye Ettori *(Manicurist)*. Howard Taylor *(Journalist)*.

Last of the Mobile Hot-shots (1969). *Director/Producer:* Sidney Lumet. *Screenplay:* Gore Vidal. *Photography:* James Wong Howe. *Music:* Quincy Jones. *Production designed by* Gene Callahan. *Associate Producer:* Jim Digangi. *Assistant Director:* Burtt Harris. Technicolor. Warner Brothers/Seven Arts. 108 minutes.

> James Coburn *(Jeb)*. Lynn Redgrave *(Myrtle)*. Robert Hooks *(Chicken)*. Perry Hayes *(George)*. Reggie King *(Rube)*. Patricia Zipprodt *(Mother)*.

Bibliography

Works by Tennessee Williams

Baby Doll, New York: New Directions; Signet paperback, 1956.

Battle of Angels, New York: Dramatists Play Service, 1975.

Camino Real, New York: New Directions, 1953; New Directions paperback, 1970.

Cat on a Hot Tin Roof and *The Milk Train Doesn't Stop Here Any More*, London: Penguin Books, 1957, 1969.

The Fugitive Kind, New York: New Directions; Signet paperback, 1960.

Garden District, London: Secker and Warburg, 1959.

The Glass Menagerie, Toronto: New Directions; The New Classics series, edited by H.D. Gutteridge, 1966, 1971.

Kindom of Earth, New York: New Directions, 1968.

"Let It All Hang Out," *New York Times*, March 4, 1973.

"Man Bring This Up Road," *Mademoiselle*, July, 1959, pp. 56-61, 102.

Memoirs, New York: Doubleday, 1975.

The Night of the Iguana, New York: New Directions; Signet paperback, 1964.

One Arm, New York: New Directions, 1948; third printing, n.d.

Period of Adjustment, New York: New Directions; Signet paperback, 1962.

"Prelude to a Comedy," *New York Times*, November 6, 1960.

The Roman Spring of Mrs. Stone, New York: New Directions; Signet paperback, 1953, 1961.

The Rose Tattoo, New York: New Directions; Signet paperback, 1955, 1956.

A Streetcar Named Desire, New York: New Directions; Signet paperback, 1951, 1955.

"A Streetcar Named Desire," photoplay (1951) published in *Film Scripts One*, edited by George P. Garrett, O.B. Hardison, Jr., and Jane R. Gelfman, New York: Appleton-Century-Crofts, 1971, pp. 330-484

"In the Script: *A Streetcar Named Desire*," *Sight and Sound*, April-June, 1952, pp.173-75.

Suddenly Last Summer, New York: New Directions; Signet paperback, 1960.

Summer and Smoke, New York: New Directions; Signet paperback, 1961.

Sweet Bird of Youth, New York: New Directions; Signet paperback, 1962.

27 Wagons Full of Cotton, New York: New Directions, 1953.

Works about Tennessee Williams

Alpert, Hollis, "In a Messel Garden," *Films and Filming*, January, 1960, pp.8, 32.

Baker, Fred, ed., *Movie People*, New York: Douglas Book Corporation, 1972.

Baker, Peter, "Cat on a Hot Tin Roof," *Films and Filming*, November, 1958, p.21.

Baker, Peter, "*Suddenly Last Summer*," *Films and Filming*, June, 1960, p.21

Basinger, Jeanine, and others, eds., *Working With Kazan*, Middleton, Conn.: Wesleyan University Press, 1973.

Bazin, André, *What Is Cinema?*, Vol. I, Berkeley and Los Angeles: University of California Press, 1967.

Bogdanovich, Peter, "An Interview with Sidney Lumet," *Film Quarterly*, Winter, 1960, pp.18-23.

Brooks, Richard, "Richard Brooks," *Movie*, No. 12 (Spring, 1965), pp.2-9, 15-16.

Calendo, John, "Tennessee Talks to John Calendo," *Interview*, April, 1973, pp. 26-28, 43.

Carey, Gary, *More About "All About Eve,"* New York: Random House, 1972; Bantam paperback, 1974.

Ciment, Michel, *Kazan on Kazan*, London: Secker and Warburg, 1973.

Conrad, Derek, "Putting on the Style," *Films and Filming*, January, 1960, pp.9, 33.

Crowther, Bosley, "Williams's Fugitives," *New York Times*, April 24, 1960.

Delahaye, Michel, "A Natural Phenomenon: Interview with Elia Kazan," *Cahiers du Cinema in English*, No. 9 (March, 1967), pp.8-40.

Dick, Bernard, *The Apostate Angel*, New York: Random House, 1974.

Durgnat, Raymond, "*This Property Is Condemned*," *Films and Filming*, November, 1966, pp.6-8.

Durgnat, Raymond, "Losey," *Films and Filming*, April, 1966, pp.26-32; May, 1966, pp.28-33.

Erens, Patricia, "Sidney Pollack: The Way We Are," *Film Comment*, September-October, 1975, pp.24-29.

Farber, Stephen, "Lumet in '69," *Sight and Sound*, Autumn, 1969, pp. 190-95.

Foster, Frederick, "Filming *The Fugitive Kind*," *American Cinematographer*, June, 1960, pp.354-55, 379-82.

Fulton, A.R., "'It's Exactly Like the Play,'" *Theater Arts*, March, 1953, pp. 78-83.

Funke, Lewis, and John E. Booth, "Williams on Williams," *Theater Arts*, January, 1962, pp.17-19, 72-73.

Gelb, Arthur, "Williams Booed at Film Preview," *New York Times*, December 8, 1959.

Gessner, Robert, *The Moving Image*, New York: E.P. Dutton, 1968.

Gow, Gordon, *Hollywood in the Fifties*, New York: A.S. Barnes, 1971.

Gow, Gordon, "Weapons," *Films and Filming*, October, 1971, pp.36-41.

Gow, Gordon, "What's Real? What's True?" *Films and Filming*, May, 1975, pp.10-16.

Gruen, John, *Close-Up*, New York: Viking, 1968.

Hewes, Henry, "The Boundaries of Tennessee," *Saturday Review*, December 29, 1956, pp.23-24.

Higham, Charles, and Joel Greenberg, *The Celluloid Muse*, Chicago: Henry Regnery, 1969; Signet paperback, 1972.

Hillier, Jim, "Kazan and Williams," *Movie*, No. 19, Winter, 1971-72, pp.17-18.

Hirsch, Foster, "Tennessee Williams," *Cinema* (Los Angeles), Spring, 1973, pp.2-8.

Jackson, Esther Merle, *The Broken World of Tennessee Williams*, Madison: University of Wisconsin Press, 1965; paperback, 1966.

Kael, Pauline, *Kiss Kiss Bang Bang*, Boston: Little Brown, 1968.

Kantor, Bernard R., Irwin Blacker, and Anne Kramer, eds., *Directors at Work*, New York: Funk and Wagnalls, 1970.

Kauffmann, Stanley, *A World on Film*, New York: Harper and Row, 1966.

Kauffmann, Stanley, *Figures of Light*, New York: Harper and Row; paperback, 1971.

Kaufman, Boris, "Filming *Baby Doll*," *American Cinematographer*, February, 1957, pp.92-93, 106-7.

Kazan, Elia, "Notebook for *A Streetcar Named Desire*," in *Directors on Directing*, edited by Toby Cole and Helen Krich Chinoy, London: Peter Owen and Vision Press, 1964.

Kazan, Elia, "Interview," *Movie*, No. 19, Winter, 1971-72, pp.1-13.

Kazan, Elia, "Dialogue on Film," *American Film*, March, 1976, pp.33-48.

Kitses, Jim, "Elia Kazan: A Structural Analysis," *Cinema* (Los Angeles), Winter, 1972-73, pp. 25-36.

Knight, Arthur, "The Williams-Kazan Axis," *Saturday Review*, December 29, 1956, pp.22-23.

Lawrenson Helen, "The Nightmare of the Iguana," *Show*, January, 1964, pp.46-49, 104-5.

Leahy, James, *The Cinema of Joseph Losey*. London: Zwemmer, 1967.

Lightman, Herb, "Uninhibited Camera," *American Cinematographer*, October, 1951, pp.400, 424, 425, 428.

Macdonald, Dwight, *On Movies*, Englewood Cliffs: Prentice-Hall, 1969.

MacMullan, Hugh, "Translating *The Glass Menagerie* to Film," *Hollywood Quarterly*, V, 1950-51, pp.14-32.

McManigal, Rod, "*Cat on a Hot Tin Roof*," *Sight and Sound*, Winter, 1958-59, p.36.

Mankiewicz, Joseph, "Measure for Measure," *Cahiers du Cinema in English*, No. 8, February, 1967, pp.28-52.

Maxwell, Gilbert, *Tennessee Williams and Friends*, Cleveland: World Publishing, 1965.

Milne, Tom, *Losey on Losey*, London: Secker and Warburg, 1967.

Murray, Edward, *The Cinematic Imagination*, New York: Frederick Ungar, 1972.

Petrie, Graham, "The Films of Sidney Lumet: Adaptation as Art," *Film Quarterly*, Winter, 1967-68, pp.9-18.

Phillips, Gene D., "Talking with John Huston," *Film Comment*, May-June, 1973, pp. 15-19.

Phillips, Gene D., "The Critical Camera of Joseph Losey," *Cinema* (Los Angeles), Spring, 1968, pp.23, 38.

"*Playboy* Interview with Tennessee Williams," *Playboy*, April, 1973, pp.69-84.

Popkin, Henry, "The Plays of Tennessee Williams," *Tulane Drama Review*, March, 1960, pp.45-64.

Quintero, José, "The Play's the Thing," *Films and Filming*, October, 1961, pp.19-21, 36-37.

Quintero, José, *If You Don't Dance They Beat You*, Boston: Little, Brown, 1974.

Reck, Tom, "Huston Meets the Eye," *Film Comment*, May-June, 1973, pp. 6-11.

Reed, Rex, *People Are Crazy Here*, New York: Delacorte Press; Dell paperback, 1975.

Reid, John Howard, "Portraying Life with Dignity," *Films and Filming*, March, 1962, pp.19-20, 44.

Reisz, Karel, "*A Streetcar Named Desire*," *Sight and Sound*, April-June, 1952, pp.171-72.

Roberts, Meade, "Williams and Me," *Films and Filming*, August, 1960, pp.7,35.

Schumach, Murray, *The Face on the Cutting Room Floor*, New York: William Morrow; da Capo paperback, 1975.

Scot, Darrin, "The Lang Touch," *American Cinematographer*, December, 1961, pp.732-33, 746-48.

Scott, Nathan, Jr., "Movies: The *Baby Doll* Furor," *The Christian Century*, January 23, 1957, pp.110-12.

Steen, Mike, *A Look at Tennessee Williams*, New York: Hawthorn, 1969.

Steen, Mike, *Hollywood Speaks*, New York: G.P. Putnam, 1974.

Tyler, Parker, "*The Fugitive Kind*," *Film Quarterly*, Summer, 1960, pp.47-49.

Tyler, Parker, *Screening the Sexes*, New York: Holt, Rinehart and Winston, 1972.

Wallis, Hal B., *Dialogue in Film,* American Film Institute, March, 1975.

Waters, Arthur B., "Tennessee Williams: Ten Years Later," *Theater Arts,* July, 1955, pp. 72-73, 96.

Weatherby, W.J., "Lonely in Upstate New York," *Manchester Guardian Weekly* (Air Edition), July 23, 1959, p. 14.

Whitehall, Richard, "Poet ... but do we know it?" *Films and Filming,* August, 1960, pp.8, 32.

Index